英语学习策略实践

庞 雅 主编

吉林出版集团股份有限公司
全国百佳图书出版单位

图书在版编目（CIP）数据

英语学习策略实践 / 庞雅主编 . -- 长春：吉林出版集团股份有限公司, 2022.11
　ISBN 978-7-5731-2790-7

　Ⅰ . ①英… Ⅱ . ①庞… Ⅲ . ①英语 – 学习方法 Ⅳ . ① H319.3

中国版本图书馆 CIP 数据核字 (2022) 第 222647 号

英语学习策略实践
YINGYU XUEXI CELÜE SHIJIAN

主　　编	庞　雅
责任编辑	沈　航
封面设计	李　伟
开　　本	710mm×1000mm　　1/16
字　　数	196 千
印　　张	12.5
版　　次	2023 年 3 月第 1 版
印　　次	2023 年 3 月第 1 次印刷
印　　刷	天津和萱印刷有限公司

出　　版	吉林出版集团股份有限公司
发　　行	吉林出版集团股份有限公司
地　　址	吉林省长春市福祉大路 5788 号
邮　　编	130000
电　　话	0431-81629968
邮　　箱	11915286@qq.com
书　　号	ISBN 978-7-5731-2790-7
定　　价	75.00 元

版权所有　翻印必究

作者简介

庞雅，女，毕业于浙江师范大学课程与教学论专业，硕士研究生学历，现为海南师范大学硕士生导师，副教授。研究方向：应用语言学，方言学，英语教学。成果：参与国家级课题1项，主持并完成省级课题2项，校级课题2项；出版学术专著2部；发表SSCI、SCI、核心论文等10余篇；曾获首届"外教社杯"全国大学英语教学大赛全国三等奖（全国十佳），2022年中国外语微课大赛全国一等奖；海南省第五批高校精品在线开放课程《综合英语（三）》主持人；海南省第二批一流本科课程《综合英语（三）》课程负责人（推荐国家级）；海南师范大学校级教学成果奖二等奖。

前 言

随着全球化的浪潮，英语的重要性被赋予了前所未有的地位，各种英语学习书籍、英语培训班等如雨后春笋，各种英语证书更是与各种荣誉挂钩，可以说在一定程度上全社会几乎达到了"我为英语狂"的状态。英语学习已经花费了每个学习者大量的财力、物力和时间，但学习的效果不尽如人意。有些学习者在小学一年级就开始英语学习，但经过12年的学习，在进入大学后，仍然是初级水平，不能发挥语言的交际功能。

长期以来，英语教学研究的重点都集中在"如何教"，对学生"如何学"关注不够，导致学生不会有效学习的后果。不仅使我国英语教育质量得不到大幅度提高，而且间接地增加了学生的学习负担，甚至会使学生觉得英语学习是一件痛苦的事情。教育的目的是使学习者成为独立、自主、有效的学习者，教师的作用不仅在于授之以"鱼"，更在于授之以"渔"，好的学习策略能增强学习者的自信心，提高学习者的学习效率，使学习者终身受益。语言学习，尤其是在非母语环境下，二语的习得更需要策略意识。英语的学习过程犹如对另外一个民族千百年的文化探寻之旅，学习策略犹如探寻之旅的路线图，有了它，虽然有跋涉的辛苦，却有方向可寻，每走出一步，都是前进，没了它，只能在漫漫长途中无助探寻，每走出的一步抑或前进，抑或后退，成功的彼岸像海市蜃楼般缥缈。有些人在旅途中放弃了，抱憾终生；有些人虽坚持不懈，却只能人在旅途，感受不到到达彼岸的欢愉。只有心怀路线图的旅人才能享受到沿途的美景，最终徜徉在瑰丽的彼岸。

本书第一章为英语口语学习策略与指导，主要从影响英语口语的原因，口语的主攻方向，口语的训练方法，四、六级口语考试介绍四个方面出发进行论述。

第二章讲述了英语阅读学习策略与指导，主要从阅读技巧解读、阅读教学与评价、阅读训练三个方面出发进行研究。第三章为英语写作学习策略与指导，对于句子写作、段落写作、篇章写作、写作技巧进行了一定的分析。第四章为英语语法学习策略与指导，主要从英语语法概述、语法的重点与难点、语法综合练习这三个方面展开。第五章是英语翻译学习策略与指导，从翻译基本理论、中西思维差异、英语翻译常用技巧三个方面展开论述。

在撰写本书的过程中，作者得到了许多专家、学者的帮助和指导，参考了大量的学术文献，在此表达真诚的感谢。本书内容系统全面，论述条理清晰、深入浅出，但由于作者水平有限，书中难免会有疏漏之处，希望广大同行及时指正。

庞雅

2022年7月

目 录

第一章　英语口语学习策略与指导 ··· 1
　　第一节　影响英语口语的原因 ··· 1
　　第二节　口语的主攻方向 ··· 2
　　第三节　口语的训练方法 ··· 4
　　第四节　四、六级口语考试介绍 ······································· 13

第二章　英语阅读学习策略与指导 ··· 31
　　第一节　阅读技巧解读 ··· 31
　　第二节　阅读教学与评价 ··· 63
　　第三节　阅读训练 ··· 71

第三章　英语写作学习策略与指导 ··· 81
　　第一节　句子写作 ··· 81
　　第二节　段落写作 ··· 94
　　第三节　篇章写作 ··· 98
　　第四节　写作技巧 ··· 110

第四章　英语语法学习策略与指导 ··· 117
　　第一节　英语语法概述 ··· 117
　　第二节　语法的重点与难点 ··· 123
　　第三节　语法综合练习 ··· 139

第五章 英语翻译学习策略与指导 …………………………………………… 145
　　第一节 翻译基本理论 ………………………………………………… 145
　　第二节 中西思维差异 ………………………………………………… 149
　　第三节 英语翻译常用技巧 …………………………………………… 154

练习参考答案 ………………………………………………………………… 177

参考文献 ……………………………………………………………………… 189

第一章 英语口语学习策略与指导

一直以来，大部分学习者在学校里接受的英语学习都是以应试为主。在多年的英语学习过程中，教师教授给学生的主要是词汇和语法方面的知识，能运用英语流畅地进行交流的学生人数并不是很多。"哑巴"英语已经成为学生学习英语最大的问题之一。随着对外开放的深化和对外交流的增多，英语口语的重要性更加凸显。语言是有声的，是一种交流工具。当今各种英语能力考试都把英语口试作为一个必考项目，因此，能否说"英语"就成了是否掌握英语的重要标志之一。本章主要介绍了影响英语口语的原因，口语的主攻方向，口语的训练方法，四、六级口语考试介绍四个方面的内容。

第一节 影响英语口语的原因

影响英语口语的原因是多方面的，因为语言交际涉及多种因素，诸如信息处理的能力、母语对第二语言的干扰、对听话人的知识态度和反应的估计等因素都会使语言产出受到影响。话语的流利性也取决于说话人的性格、自信心、健康及对情况的熟悉程度、准备的充分与否等许多因素的影响。在此，大体将其归纳为以下几个因素：

一、认知因素

学习者的知识水平对他的语言口语能力起着至关重要的作用。从语言输出的心理过程来看，学习者首先通过学习了解一定目的语的语音、词汇、句法知识和规则。在有了交际需要的时候，学习者先要在储存于大脑的语言词汇库中选取合适的词语，并按一定的语义和语法规则把它们有机地编排起来，组织好的语言码再由大脑协调发音器官转化为声音发出。这一编码的过程实际上是说话人用内部言语进行言语计划的过程。显然，要说得快而且流畅、连贯，说话人头脑中要存储丰富的语言知识，包括语言材料和规则。总而言之，语言知识的内化程度是最根本的因素之一，是实现口语流利的一个前提。

二、心理因素

在知识水平相当的情况下，学习动因比较高的人会产生促进性心理焦虑，而学习动因较低的人会产生促退性心理焦虑。前者在语言发出时会努力表现自己，尽量提高口语的流利程度。焦虑、恐惧、迟疑等心理现象会干扰话语计划与发出的全过程，会直接影响英语口语的流利程度。

三、环境因素

语言环境是指说话的时间、地点、对象等客观具体环境。一般人在稳定的自然环境下习得第一语言，或者在这样的环境下习得第二语言，都不会有太大的困难，即使不经过语法知识的学习也可以完成语法系统的内化；缺乏稳定的语言环境则完全不同，即使通过课堂教学能掌握英语语法规则，但英语达到母语般流利程度的也很少。

第二节　口语的主攻方向

根据前面提到的影响口语的因素，可以确定口语学习的四大主攻方向，即语音、词汇、句型、文化。

一、语音

学好英语要先过语音关。正确的语音不仅使听力受益，而且还是英语交际成功的保障，也是展示自身形象的重要方面。然而，要改变自己的乡土音和外国腔，掌握良好的英语语音、语调，不是一件容易的事，除了需要大量的实践和练习外，还需要掌握英语语音、语调的基本知识，只有这样，训练起来才能做到胸有成竹。

二、词汇

有的学习者可能会有这样的疑问：自己的口语已经不错了，可为什么在外国人面前还是无法顺畅交流呢？答案很简单：词汇量积累不够。谈到积累，学习者常会走入误区——认为积累的词汇量越多越好，句式越高级复杂越好。其实不然，当在和外国人交流时，英美人士多用简单的词汇、俚语来进行日常交流——这也是英语口语学习的最高境界。如 get 一词堪称口语中的"钻石级"词汇，一词多义，使用极其频繁。比如，打球时觉得累了，我们可能会说 feel tired，但这种说法并不如 get tired 来得地道。还有一个非常简单但并不是每个人都能说得出的句子：Do you know how to get there（不用 go there）？所以在词汇的掌握方面，应该注重词汇的实用性和功能性。抓住那些简单而地道的词语，深刻理解它们的功能和用法，就可以掌握口语用词的精髓。

三、句型

第三个着力点是口语中的句型，它好比数学中的公式，只要掌握了其中的一类，就可以进行部分替换，改装出多个不同的句子。那如何有效地掌握句型呢？我们可以对不同的句型进行归纳整理，了解并记忆各个句型的功能及其适用的场景。通俗地说，就是在什么地方，遇到什么人就要说什么话。比如，在 greeting 的场景中，我们就要说诸如 How are you/How are you doing/What's up 之类的话，而不能不顾情境抛出一句像"Where are you going"这样不符合英美习惯的话。整理出不同句型的不同功能，对其进行记忆和练习，将十分有助于达到英语脱口而出的境界。

四、文化

语言作为一种社会交际的工具，其产生和发展是离不开社会背景和历史条件的。所以，每一种语言本身都是一种文化的体现。对这种文化的了解必然有助于语言的学习。所以在学习口语时，不仅要尽可能多地掌握语言知识，补充大量的口语词汇和句型，还要深刻地挖掘语言背后的文化背景。多数的学习者在长期学习英语的过程中，由于缺乏一定的英语环境，容易形成中式思维，闹出"中式英语"的笑话。比方说，一名男士称赞一位女士："Today you look very beautiful！"（今天您可真漂亮啊！）这位女士立刻谦虚地回答："Where！Where！"（哪里！哪里！）结果对方尴尬地说："Everywhere！"（全身都漂亮！）事实上，在西方交际文化中，对于社交场合上的这种恭维话，我们只需回答 Thanks（谢谢）即可。因此，为提高口语表达的准确性，平时应该多了解西方文化，包括经济、价值观、时间概念、空间关系、行动、态度等，对比中西方交际方式和思维差异。与英语国家文化接触量的多少将影响语言学习者将外在的语言输入转化为内在的语言纳入的成功程度，只有多接触英语国家的文化才能逐渐使自己的英语口语符合英语国家的表达习惯。但学习者在国内生活，不具备很好的英语文化浸润条件，那又该如何了解英语文化呢？最直观的方式便是大量观看英文电影、电视剧。在这里，推荐 Friends（《六人行》，又名《老友记》），这是一部情景喜剧，囊括了美国生活的各个方面。如果能研究并掌握里面所有的对话，就一定能和外国人自由交流。

第三节 口语的训练方法

一、口语训练指导原则

（一）"输入输出"理论

学、念、背课文是输入，是基础；将课文单词、词组、句子融会贯通，灵活地用出来、讲出来是输出，是技能。

（二）"中英转换"理论

我们要认清中英文的异同之处，彻底熟悉并掌握中英文之间的转换规律、要领、特点、具体方法和技巧，达到中英文间自如转换的最高境界。

（三）"口译核心"理论

达到中英文间自如转换的最直接、最快捷的途径就是集中进行大量中英文句子之间的口头翻译。在教师的指导下，学习者可以熟悉并掌握中英文转换的规律、特点、方法和技巧。学习者若多积累一些词汇量，每天用顺译法口译（中译英），长此以往，学习者的口语表达水平一定会实现质的飞跃。

二、口语训练须冲过 12 道大关

口语学习是个系统工程，必须冲过"语音、词汇、听力、开口、组句、质效、转换、找话、范围、正误、深度、漂亮"12 道大关，如果只掌握其中一两种片面的技巧是远远不够的，必须冲破每一道大关才能拥有一口流利的英语口语。

（一）冲过语音关

达到发音标准，正确熟练拼读单词，会利用读音规则促进单词拼读，轻重音分明，能正确地运用平调、升调和降调，能熟练流畅地朗读句子、会话和长篇发言。

（二）冲过词汇关

能将学过的单词用出来，掌握同义词的选择规律，掌握常用多义词的不同含义的运用，学会大量的词语搭配，包括众多的惯用搭配。

（三）冲过听力关

能够轻松听懂正常语速的英语会话和长篇发言（英语电影、英语电视剧较特殊，其背景有噪音，语音有时也较模糊，干扰较大，不宜作为听力检验标准）。

（四）冲过开口关

要明白犯错是不可避免的，犯错是进步的阶梯，不在乎暂时的小错误，并积极改正，敢于开口讲，乐于讲英语。

（五）冲过组句关

掌握组句总规律"顺译法"，熟练处理疑问句和少数倒装句的结构，掌握快速摆放前置、后置定语和句尾状语的技巧。

（六）冲过质效关

掌握并运用一整套口语突击技巧，提高学习效率和信心。

（七）冲过转换关

在中英文转换过程中，大部分词语搭配、句子结构是相同相近的，可以直接转换。懂得并学会那些（少数）不能直接转换的内容的处理方法和技巧，尤其是像"胸有成竹（confident）""给他点儿颜色看看（teach him a lesson）""吃苦（endure hardships）""吃亏（suffer losses）""吃醋（be jealous）"等成语、习语、俗语的转换要领和技巧，达到中英文间全面自如的转换。

（八）冲过找话关

掌握会话时选材、选要点、要点发挥、段落发展的基本方法，学会"往细处说"的技巧，达到就任何一个普通的话题都能够深入细致地交谈30分钟以上的程度。

（九）冲过范围关

掌握成倍扩展法、直接冲高法、纵横神侃法、出口成章法，并利用这四大技巧进行丰富广泛的训练，不仅能谈论日常生活，还能深入广泛地谈论工作、学习、各种社会问题。

（十）冲过正误关

用成片扫错法、盯异法等方法成串、成片地快速扫除各类常见错误，实现意思表达、语法、措辞方面的正确无误。

（十一）冲过深度关

通过对"长句驾驭""复杂内容整理""抽象深奥内容表达"进行有针对的训练，能快速达到驾驭高难度英语的高级水平。

（十二）冲过漂亮关

弄清什么是漂亮的英语，采用有针对性的美化方法，在语流、选词、搭配、表达方式、句子结构调整、选材、层次调整、脉络梳理、逻辑连贯、生动性、清晰度、内容提炼、说服力、比喻、排比、拟人化、趣味性等方面进行改进训练，快速全面美化口语。

三、口语的具体训练方法

首先要了解问题所在，才有可能对症下药，制定切实可行的方案，采用有效的学习策略。当我们了解到英语口语受影响的原因后，就会有的放矢地采取有效措施，从语言学习策略着手，克服阻碍口语进步的各种因素，利用行之有效的方法流利地说英语。

一般来说，衡量一个人口语水平高低主要看以下几个方面：语音、语调是否正确，口齿是否清楚；流利程度，语法是否正确，用词是否恰当，是否符合英语表达习惯；内容是否充实，逻辑是否清晰。

针对以上标准，采取相应的训练方法，大致可分作两个阶段。

（一）准备阶段

准备阶段的目的是训练正确的语音、语调，提高流利程度，培养英语语感。同时，通过各种方式，如阅读、做练习题、看英语电影等来扩大词汇量。掌握英语的习惯表达方式，扩大知识面，训练英语逻辑思维能力。准备会话前，要对常用的词（组）、短语等熟练掌握，"熟练"是与人会话的前提，只有熟练，在会话时才能流利。熟练的标准就是要达到脱口而出。

1. 模仿

模仿包括两方面重点：语音和语调。关于"发音"，要训练对每个元音、辅音进行准确的发音。关于"语调",尽管很多时候可能比语音更重要,但这一点最容易被忽略,这是模仿的重点。模仿是学习英语的主要方法。

模仿的原则:一要大声模仿。这一点很重要,模仿时要大大方方,清清楚楚,口形要到位。在刚开始模仿时,速度要慢一些,以便把音发到位。把音发准了以后,再加快速度,直到能用正常语速把句子轻松地说出来。大声模仿的目的是使口腔的肌肉充分活动起来,改变多年来肌肉形成的汉语发音的运动模式,使嘴与大脑逐渐协调起来,建立起新的口腔肌肉的运动模式(英语发音的运动模式)。若在练习时总是小声地在嗓子眼儿里发音,一旦需要大声说话时,就可能发不准音,出现错误。二要随时准备纠正自己说不好的单词、短语等。有了这种意识,在模仿时就不会觉得单调、枯燥,才能主动、有意识、有目的地去模仿,这种模仿才是真正的模仿,才能达到模仿的目的,也就是要用心揣摩、体会。三要坚持长期模仿。一般来说,纯正优美的语音、语调不是短期模仿所能达到的,对于有英语基础的人学说美语也是如此,对于习惯说汉语的人学说英语更是如此。语音、语调的过渡需要一段时间,时间的长短取决于学习者的专心程度。练习模仿是件苦差事,常常会练得口干舌燥,此时一定要坚持。

模仿要达到什么程度才算模仿好了呢?简单地说就是要"像",如果能够达到"是"就更好了。"像"是指模仿者的语音、语调等都很接近所模仿的语言,"是"就是不仅在语音、语调等方面都很接近所模仿的声音,而且非常逼真,连嗓音也基本一样,简直可以以假乱真。

模仿的具体方法:第一步,模仿单词的语音。模仿时要有板有眼,口型要正确,口腔肌肉要充分调动起来。刚开始模仿时,速度不要过快,要慢速模仿,以便把音发到位。待把音发准了以后,再加快速度,用正常语速反复多说几遍,直到脱口而出。对于自己读不准或较生疏的单词要反复多听几遍,然后再反复模仿。要及时在读错的单词下面做标记、提示,写下正确的音标、发音注意事项、自己的发音心得,争取读得自然。学习者可以反复读,如果有条件,录下自己的发音,将自己的发音和模仿对象进行对比,发现两者之间的差距。第二步,模仿词组的读法。有了第一步的基础,这一步就容易多了。重点要放在熟练程度和流利程度上,要多练一下连读、同化等语音技巧。第三步,段落及篇章模仿，重点在于提高流利程度。要提高口腔肌肉的反应速度，使肌肉和大脑更加协调。这时可欣赏演讲名篇等，向口语流利后的更高目标努力。学习者能在众人面前慷慨陈词，调动起听者的情绪，成为好的演讲者是口语表达的最高境界。

在进行模仿练习时要注意一个问题，就是害羞心理。害羞心理一方面源于性格，一般性格内向的人，讲话时易小声，这对学习英语语音、语调很不利，要注意克服。另一方面源于自卑心理，总以为自己英语水平太差，不敢开口，尤其是当与口语水平比自己高的人对话时，更容易出现这种情况。克服这种心理障碍是学好口语的前提。

2. 复述

学英语离不开记忆，记忆不是死记硬背，要有灵活性。复述就是一种很好的自我训练口语，记忆单词、句子的形式。复述有两种常见的方法：一种是阅读后复述，一种是听录音或看视频后复述。后种方法更好些，这种方法既练听力，又练口语表达能力，同时，可以提高注意力和听的效果，而且还可以提高记忆力，克服听完就忘的毛病。

复述的具体方法是要循序渐进，可由一两句开始，听完后用自己的话（英语）把所听到的内容说出来，一遍复述不下来，可多听几遍，越练需要听的次数就越少。在刚开始练习时，因语言表达能力、技巧等方面的原因，复述往往接近于背诵，但在基础逐渐打起来后，就会慢慢放开。在保证语言正确的前提下，复述可有越来越大的灵活性，如改变句子结构，删去一些不太有用或过难的东西，长段可以缩短，甚至仅复述大意或作内容概要。

复述的内容要有所选择。一般来说，所选资料的内容要具体生动，有明确的情节，生词量不要太大。可选那些知识性强的小短文，开始时可以练习复述小故事，有了基础后，复述的题材可扩展开些。

复述表面上看进度慢，实际上对英语综合能力的培养很有帮助。如果时间比较充足，可以在口头复述的基础上，再用笔头复述一下，这样做可以加深掌握语言的精确程度，提高书面表达能力。

3. 背诵

背诵是学习英语的一种有效方法，是知识输入的一种有效途径，不但可以帮助学习者掌握大量的英语基础知识，而且还可以培养丰富的语感。在学习过程中，学习者们一定要掌握科学的方法，提高背诵的效率。

背诵的具体方法是：首先，要树立理解背诵的观念。随着年龄的增长，学习者的理解能力逐渐增强，简单机械的背诵不但费时费力，而且容易产生厌倦的情绪，因而学习效率很低，这就要求不要死记硬背，而要在理解的基础上进行背诵，以提高背诵速度，增强学习效果。其次，扫除语音障碍。单词读不准音或不会读是背诵的一大障碍。一篇课文中如果有太多生疏的单词，就会影响学习者背诵的信心。为此，可以通过听录音或听教师的示范朗读来帮助自己找出这样的单词，纠正发音。同时，还要注意句子的语调、不完全爆破、重弱读等语音现象，增强诵读的节奏，提高背诵的效率。再次，抓关键词语。在背诵时，有些学习者习惯逐字地背诵，把一个完整的句子弄得支离破碎，影响了背诵的效果。众所周知，句子是由短语构成的，不同的短语构成不同的意群，在读的时候，应该按照完整的意群进行停顿，保持句子形式和意思上的完整性，这样在我们记忆中也是一个完整的句子，然后再排除语法上的困难。课文中那些句子较长、结构较复杂的句子是学习者最难理解和背诵的。对于这样的句子，可以先分析其结构类型：简单句，分清主、谓、宾、定、状、补；复合句，弄明白是哪一种类型的复合句。同时，还要注意句与句之间的联系，这样就可以迅速理解句子的意思，背诵起来就容易多了。最后，把课文分层进行背诵，根据课文的中心内容划分层次，化整为零，化难为易，逐层背诵，直到通背全文。

4. 选择适当的教材

在选择适用的口语教材时，先选用一两种国内出版的教科书，这类教材内容会紧密结合我们的日常习惯，题材比较贴近生活，便于开口练习，随着能力的提高，可以过渡到使用国外编写的课本。这些书的内容虽不完全切合我国的生活实际，但利用它们不但可以练习准确的发音，还能了解外国的风土人情。

5. 注意积累

口语的学习和练习，需要经常收集并熟练掌握英美人民会话时常用的习语和特有的表达方式。有些习语和表达方式在口语教科书上能够找到，也有不少是找不到的，同时不断有新词汇出现，把重要的习语抄在一个专门的笔记本上，经常反复练习，长此以往，英语的口语表达能力就会更生动、更丰富。特别注意短语（词组）和小词的运用，中国式的英语，尤其是口语，有一个很大的缺点，就是学生喜欢用大词，而真正地道的英语口语充满着短小、活泼、生动的短语，富有生气，这些短语大部分由小词构成。

在口语学习中要尊重英语国家的谈话方式和语言习惯，逐步适应并掌握语言习惯，不能用自己的观点和方式去评判这些习惯，更不能去改变它。我们也不能以自己的思维方式和表达方法与外国人对话，而应该尽量考虑到英美国家人民的生活和语言表达方式。

（二）实践阶段

这个阶段主要进行大量的会话练习，主要有以下方法：

1. 寻找伙伴

在日常的学习生活中可寻找学伴一起练习，根据不同的情景进行题材广泛的练习。英语角是个不错的地方，在那里我们不但可以练习口语，还可以交流英语学习经验，开阔视野，提高英语学习兴趣。更要走出家门，主动寻找口语教师和对话伙伴，积极参加社会上的各种英语交流活动，参与由英语爱好者组成的自学者团体，即使没有英国人和美国人当交流对象，也可以用英语进行会话和专题讨论，互相学习、矫正和提高，假以时日，就一定能做连贯的发言和交流。

2. 口译简易读物

如果找不到学伴或参加英语角的机会很少也没有关系，还有很多种方法可以自己练习口语。比如，通过自己对自己讲英语来创造英语环境，尝试口译汉英对照（或英汉对照）的小说或其他读物，这种方法非常有效且很容易坚持。首先读汉语部分，其次逐句直接口译成英文，完成一小段后，去看书上的对应英文部分，并与自己的口译进行比较，从而发现自己口译的错误、缺点和进步。需要注意的是，在开始的时候，要选择较简单的读物，且应大量做练习，只做一两篇效果是不明显的。开始可能较慢，费时较多，但要坚持住，整体上这是一个进步的过程。

高级阶段要计时练习，以加快反应速度和口语流利度。

对于那些记忆力不好，做复述练习或背诵课文力不从心，或者由于词汇量太小觉得直接做口译太难的学习者来说，这样做可以非常有效地解决这个问题：先学习英文课文，在通篇理解透彻后，再来看汉语译文，把汉语译文口译回英文，这样等于既做复述练习，又做口译（语）练习，可谓一举两得。

这样做的好处有以下六点：

第一，自己就可以练习口语，想练多久就练多久。

第二，始终有一位"高级教师"指出自己的不足和错误——英文原文。

第三，题材范围极广，可以突破自己的思维禁锢，为自己的语料库补充各种内容，打破谈话的局限。

第四，选择自己有兴趣的小说、幽默故事或好的短文阅读，挖掘出平时很难发现的地道的英语用法。

第五，对所学知识和所犯错误印象深刻。

第六，翻译水平加强了，口语表达力提高了。

3. 听译法——角色互换

三人一组，模拟翻译实战，一人讲汉语，一人讲英语，一人做翻译，练习一段时间后互换角色。这是一种非常好的翻译训练方法，也是相互学习、取长补短的方法，而且可以提高反应速度和能力。此法的高级阶段为同声传译，我们可以在听广播、看电视或开会时，把所听内容口译成英文。

4. 口语作文和 3 分钟训练法

先找好一个题目，做 1 分钟的口语作文，同时将其录音。之后听录音，找出不足和错误，就此题目再做 2 分钟的口语作文，同样录音，再听并找出不足与进步，继续做 3 分钟口语作文。这是高级口语训练，效果不俗。

Attitude is everything! 态度决定一切！在做一件事之前，如果我们自卑、彷徨，就会离成功越来越远。口语学习也是如此，口语学习有两大支柱——信心和恒心，相信自己通过练习一定会提高说好英语的能力，但一定要有心理准备，因为口语学习是一个长期甚至有点儿枯燥的过程。

"三分钟热度""三天打鱼，两天晒网"最后都会无所收效，只有循序渐进，才能有所进步。同时也要认识到要熟练掌握说英语的能力,必须在特定的条件下进行大量实践,课上练习口语的时间远远不够,在纯汉语环境中练习英语口语需要学习者自己创造环境和条件。

第四节　四、六级口语考试介绍

一、四级口语考试介绍

(一)官方样题概要

官方样题概要如表1-4-1所示。

表1-4-1　四级口语考试官方样题概要

任务	任务名称	任务描述	时间
热身	自我介绍(Self-introduction)	考生做简短的自我介绍	每人20秒
1	短文朗读(Read aloud)	考生经过准备后,朗读一篇短文	准备:45秒 答题:1分钟
2	简短回答(Question & answer)	考生回答两个与所朗读的短文有关的问题	答题:每题20秒
3	个人陈述(Individual presentation)	考生在经过准备后,根据所给提示做1分钟的发言	准备:45秒 答题:1分钟
4	小组互动(Pair work)	两位考生在经过准备后,根据设定的情景和任务进行交谈	准备:1分钟 答题:3分钟

(二)考官评分标准

1. 评分等级描述

四级口语考试评分标准共分为A、B、C、D四个等级。

(1) A级

①能用英语就熟悉的话题进行交谈,基本没有困难。

②能就熟悉的话题连贯地发表意见和看法。

③能清晰、流利地叙述或描述一般性事件和现象。

（2）B级

①能用英语就熟悉的话题进行交谈，虽有些困难，但不影响交际。

②能就熟悉的话题作较连贯的发言。

③能较清晰、流利地叙述或描述一般性事件和现象。

（3）C级

①能用英语就熟悉的话题进行简单的交谈。

②能就熟悉的话题做简短的发言。

③能简单地叙述或描述一般性事件和现象。

（4）D级

尚不具备英语口头交际能力。

2. 能力解析

按照上文A～D四个级别的评分标准划分，A是大学英语四级口语考试中的最佳等级，以下逐条分析A级的具体要求：

（1）能用英语就熟悉的话题进行交谈，基本没有困难

这项能力要求考生掌握与人、事、地、物等话题相关的词汇。在答题时间上，自我介绍和每道简短回答题均为20秒，短文朗读和个人陈述均为1分钟，小组互动部分为3分钟。按照英语正常交流的语速，考生的语速最好达到1秒钟说两个或更多单词。所以根据各部分的时间设置可以推算，自我介绍和简短回答题的答案应不少于40个单词（20秒）、短文朗读和个人陈述的答案应不少于120个单词（1分钟），小组互动部分的答案应不少于360个单词（3分钟）。

（2）能就熟悉的话题连贯地发表意见和看法

关于这项能力的培养，同学们应熟悉本书列出的话题，并能够按照句型找到"态度＋情感"的表述模式，即能够把控when to comment, what to comment and how to comment（何时评价、说什么、如何说）。

（3）能清晰、流利地叙述或描述一般性事件和现象

同学们应熟悉本书模拟题和自测题中列出的话题，并善于总结关于"事实"的表述模式，学习如何描述事物或现象，并适当添加时间、地点和方式等细节信息。另外，在小组互动部分，除了以上"事实＋态度＋情感"的话题引申外，还

要注意对搭档所说的内容进行反馈,也就是"反馈+新话题"的模式。有了"反馈"和"新话题",对话才能顺利进行,并言之有物、言之有序。

二、六级口语考试介绍

(一)官方样题概要

大学英语六级口语考试采用计算机化的考试形式。模拟考官及试题均呈现在计算机屏幕上,试题材料采用文字或画面提示(如图画、图表、照片等)。考生由计算机系统随机编排为两人一组。考生在计算机上进行考生与模拟考官、考生与考生之间的互动,考试总时间约18分钟。

考试内容及流程如表1-4-2所示。

表1-4-2 六级口语考试官方样题概要

部分	时间	题型	说明
第一部分(Part 1)	约3分钟	自我介绍和回答	自我介绍:每位考生20秒,两位考生依次进行 回答问题:每位考生30秒,两位考生同时作答
第二部分(Part 2)	约10分钟	陈述和讨论	个人陈述:考生准备1分钟后,根据所给提示作答,每位考生1分30秒,两位考生依次进行 两人讨论:两位考生就指定的话题进行约4分30秒的讨论
第三部分(Part 3)	约2分钟	问答	问答:由考官进一步提问,每位考生45秒,两位考生同步作答

注:根据全国大学英语四、六级考试官方网站提供的样题以及口试录像视频,两人讨论的时间为4分30秒,但是2016年修订版的《全国大学英语四、六级考试大纲》对两人讨论的时间描述为3分钟。为了给各位考生提供更多的参考语料,本书模拟试题的两人讨论版块均按照4分30秒的时长设置。

(二)考官评分标准

1. 人工评分标准

六级口语考试全部采用人工评分,总分为15分,成绩报道时转换为A、B、C、D四个等级。

人工评分基于以下三项标准，每个单项满分为5分，评分标准描述如下：

（1）准确性和范围

"准确性"指考生的语音、语调以及所使用的语法和词汇的准确程度，"范围"指考生使用的词汇和语法结构的复杂度和丰富度。

① 5分

A. 语法和词汇基本正确。

B. 表达过程中词汇丰富、语法结构较为复杂。

C. 发音较好，但允许有一些不影响理解的母语口音。

② 4分

A. 语法和词汇有一些错误，但未严重影响交际。

B. 表达过程中词汇较丰富。

C. 发音尚可。

③ 3分

A. 语法和词汇有错误，且有时会影响交际。

B. 表达过程中词汇不丰富，语法结构较简单。

C. 发音有缺陷，有时会影响交际。

④ 2分

A. 语法和词汇有相当多的错误，以致交际时常中断。

B. 表达过程中因缺乏词汇和语法结构而严重影响交际。

C. 发音较差。

⑤ 1分

不描述。

（2）话语长短和连贯性

"话语长短"指考生对整个考试中的交际所做的贡献、讲话的多少，"连贯性"指考生能进行较长时间的、语言连贯的发言。

① 5分

能进行较长时间的发言，语言连贯，组织思想和搜寻词语时偶尔出现停顿，但不影响交际。

② 4 分

A. 能进行较连贯的发言，但多数发言较简短。

B. 组织思想和搜寻词语时频繁出现停顿，有时会影响交际。

③ 3 分

A. 发言简短。

B. 组织思想和搜寻词语时频繁出现较长时间且影响交际的停顿，但能基本完成交际任务。

④ 2 分

发言简短且毫无连贯性，基本不能进行正常交际。

⑤ 1 分

不描述。

（3）灵活性和适切性

"灵活性"指考生应付不同场景和话题的能力，"适切性"指考生根据不同场合选用适当确切的语言的能力。

① 5 分

A. 能自如地应对不同场景和话题。

B. 能积极地参与讨论。

C. 语言的使用总体上能与语境、功能和目的相适应。

② 4 分

A. 能较自如地应对不同场景和话题。

B. 能较积极地参与讨论。

C. 语言的使用基本上能与语境、功能和目的相适应。

③ 3 分

A. 不能积极参与讨论。

B. 有时不能适应话题或内容的转换。

④ 2 分

不能参与讨论。

⑤1分

不描述。

2. 能力等级描述

（1）A级

①能用英语就一般性话题进行深入的交谈。

②能清晰、流利地表达个人意见、情感、观点等。

③能详细地陈述事实、理由和描述事件、现象等。

（2）B级

①能用英语就一般性话题进行较深入的交谈。

②能较清晰、连贯地表达个人意见、情感、观点等。

③能较详细地陈述事实、理由和描述事件、现象等。

（3）C级

①能用英语就一般性话题进行简单的交谈。

②能基本表达个人建议、情感、观点等。

③能简单地陈述事实、理由和描述事件、现象等。

（4）D级

尚不具备基本的英语口头交际能力。

三、四、六级口语考试技巧

本书旨在帮助应试者在四、六级口语考试中做到内容翔实、逻辑严谨、表述地道、用词丰富、句式多变、单复数和时态语态使用准确，同时能使用正确的英文语调。如果用一句话总结令人满意的口语，那就是在语音上能和四、六级听力录音一样优美，在逻辑上能和四、六级阅读一样舒展。这样的口语就能真正"走出课堂，走向社会"。

（一）句子的"扩张原则"

正如一个单词可以通过加前缀或后缀构成另一个单词，一个句子的前面也可以"导入"一个背景或者"让步"一下，后面可以"补入"一个结果或者"附加"

一个条件或原因，中间也可以"插入"解释性、延展性的信息，从而丰富句子的内容，达到"扩张"的目的。

1. "导入"的例子

Acting on his recommendation, I have decided to practice English regularly.

根据他的建议，我决定定期练习英语。

As a matter of fact, John came into the room while we were talking about him.

事实是，约翰走进房间的时候，我们正在谈论他。

Unlike the others, I have a poor sense of direction.

不像其他人，我的方向感很差。

Apart from being too large, the color of the clothes does not suit me.

除了太大，这些衣服的颜色也不适合我。

2. "补入"的例子

Thank you all for coming to class at such a short notice.

通知得太仓促，谢谢大家来上课。

We will agree to let you pass as long as you prove you are a student.

只要能证明你是学生，我们就同意让你通过。

You are free to come and go at will.

你来去自由。

The rules apply to everyone, without exception.

规定适用于所有人，无一例外。

3. "插入"的例子

The novel, I think, is both interesting and instructive.

我认为这本小说既有趣又有教育意义。

She, like thousands of others, is greatly fascinated by this work of art.

正如成千上万的其他人一样，她也被这件艺术品深深地迷住了。

His family tragedy, believe it or not, did happen at last.

不管你信不信，他的家庭悲剧最终还是发生了。

When he got there, he found, however, that the weather was too bad.

但是，到达那里的时候，他发现天气太糟糕了。

We can, frankly, do nothing about it.

坦率地说，我们无能为力。

（二）段落"面上铺开"的技巧

所谓"面上铺开"就是"换言之"，同一个意思可以用不同的单词和句子表达，或者从不同的角度描述。比如，谈到 mobile phone 时，在展开阐述的过程中不免会多次提及这个中心词，为避免重复，我们可以用其近义词替代，如 handset、cell phone，或用其上义词 a useful tool、a great invention 替代，也可以用其下义词 smartphone，或者诸如 it、one、this 之类的代词来指代。比如，在谈到 mobile phone 很便利时，我们可以说 Cell phone has proven to be a useful tool. No one can deny its convenience. It is so handy, we can get things done without leaving home and get instant feedback on the spot with an iPhone, which saves us a lot of time, energy and in many cases, money. Thanks to the great invention, our life is much easier。如此一来，用词多变，符合英文简洁的特点。

（三）段落"点上深入"的方法

任何交流都是有着特定目的（主题）并逐渐深入的。这里所列的方法主要针对大学英语四、六级口语考试。因为考试有时间限制和固定评分标准，因此同学们在考试中的交流点到即可。具体实施可以分为三个步骤：阐述事实、评价、表达情感。如果话题关于食物，首先可以阐述有关食物的事实，比如，食物的种类：vegetable、fruit、meat、seafood 等，食物的烹饪方法：fried、baked、steamed、boiled、sauteed、grilled、braised、raw 等，食物的口味：sweet、spicy、sour、savory 等；其次对食物进行评价，如 healthy、tasty、good for your stomach or skin 等；最后表达个人的喜好和感受。这样就从事实、评价、情感三个角度阐述了一个主题。图片陈述和对话部分尤其要注意思路深入，遵循"面上铺开，点上深入"的原则，同学们一定会有不一样的表现。

（四）常见反馈方式

1.Agree（同意）

This is an exciting city.

—Absolutely/Exactly/Definitely.

—You bet.

—It sure is.

—True.

2.Disagree（不同意）

I think bungee jumping is exciting.

—I see what you mean, but won't it be dangerous?

—You are right, but what will your parents say?

—Perhaps, but I can't help thinking that if the elastic is broken.

—True, but I am afraid it's not cheap.

—Honestly / Frankly, I think it's a bit risky.

3.Clarify（确认）

There is a shopping mall near the theater.

—I am sorry, a shopping mall, did you say?

—I am sorry, I didn't quite follow you, could you please say it again?

4.Positive feedback（积极反馈）

I have passed my CET-4!

—Good to hear that!

—Happy for you!

—Lucky you!

—That's amazing / wonderful / fabulous / perfect!

—Congratulations!

5.Negative feedback（消极反馈）

I lost my wallet.

—Sorry to hear that.

—Poor you.

—That's terrible.

—What a pity!

四、大学英语口语考试模拟题及详解

（一）Self-introduction

Hello, welcome to the CET Spoken English Test-Band Four. We wish you both good luck today. Now let's begin with self-introductions.

Candidate A, would you please start?（考生 A 先回答，时间 20 秒）

Thank you. Candidate B, now it's your turn.（然后考生 B 回答，时间 20 秒）

Thank you. OK, now that we know each other, let's go on.

参考答案

考生 A：

Hello, my name is Kelly. I am a student of Hefei University of Technology. I am from Hefei, the capital city of Anhui Province. My hobbies are various, such as running at night, watching entertainment show on the Internet and so on. As a common girl, I like gossiping hot issues and playing mobile games on my cell phone. In addition to the above-mentioned, in my spare time, I am willing to do housework and cook some food for my family. Last but not least, my ambition is so simple that I want to live in the moment. That's all, thank you.

考生 B：

I'm Jerry, a college student at Beijing Institute of Technology. I grew up in Beijing, the capital city of China. I love my hometown because it is a metropolis which is full of vigor and vitality. My hobby is playing different games, including video games and card games. When it comes to study, I am good at biology but poor in math. By the way, I am interested in science. I will be glad to find someone to chat with me in this field.

精彩表达

various/ˈveriəs/a. 各种各样的；多方面的

entertainment show 娱乐节目

gossip/ˈgɑːsɪp/n. 小道传闻；绯闻

ambition/æmˈbɪʃn/n. 野心；抱负

vigor/ˈvɪɡər/n. 活力；精力

vitality/vaɪˈtæləti/n. 活力，生气；生命力，生动性

when it comes to 当谈到 / 提及……

by the way 顺便说一句

（二）Task 1　Read Aloud

In this task, you are to read aloud a short passage. You will have 45 seconds to go over the passage and 1 minute to read it aloud. Now here is the passage.

（屏幕显示以下文字）

The historical definition of a computer is a device that can help in computation. Computation includes counting, calculating, adding, subtracting, etc. The modern definition of a computer is a little different. Today's computers store, manipulate, and analyze many kinds of information. Historically, the first computers are very interesting. The first computer may actually have been located in Great Britain, at Stonehenge. It is a man-made circle of large stones. People used it to measure the weather and predict the change of seasons. Another ancient computer is the abacus. The early Chinese, Romans, Greeks, and Egyptians used this device to count and calculate. Although they are no longer used, these early computers provide fascinating insight into early computers and computing.

（考生准备时间 45 秒）

Now please begin to read on hearing the beep.

（考生 A 和 B 同时回答，时间 1 分钟）

高分秘诀

本段文字介绍了计算机的两类定义及其功能。从历史上来看，计算机是用于帮助人们进行加、减、乘、除的计算设备。而在当代，计算机的定义发生了许多变化，其主要目的是储存、管理、分析各类信息。文章最后介绍了两种古代计算机，一种是位于大不列颠的巨石阵，另一种是算盘，历史上曾被广泛用于中国、罗马、希腊、埃及等国。由于出现了一些专业词汇，文章难度稍大，考生在朗读时要注意专业词汇的读音，平时还是要广泛阅读各类英语文章。

The historical definition of a computer/ is a device/ that can help in computation. Computation includes counting, calculating, adding, subtracting, etc. The modern definition of a computer/ is a little different. Today's computers store, manipulate, and analyze many kinds of information. Historically, the first computers are very interesting. The first computer may actually have been located/ in Great Britain, at Stonehenge. It is a man-made circle of large stones. People used it/ to measure the weather and predict the change/ of seasons. Another ancient computer is the abacus. The early Chinese, Romans, Greeks, and Egyptians used this device/ to count and calculate. Although they are no longer used, these early computers provide fascinating insight/ into early computers and computing.

精彩表达

calculate/ˈkælkjuleɪt/v. 计算；预测；认为

subtract/səbˈtrækt/v. 减去；扣掉

manipulate/məˈnɪpjuleɪt/v. 操作；操纵

Stonehenge/ˌstəʊnˈhendʒ/n. 巨石阵

abacus/ˈæbəkəs/n. 算盘

Egyptian/iˈdʒɪpʃn/n. 埃及人

fascinating/ˈfæsɪneɪtɪŋ/a. 吸引人的

（三）Task 2　Question and Answer

In this task, you are to answer two questions. For each question, you will have 20 seconds to respond. Please start speaking on hearing the beep.

（问题文字不显示在屏幕上）

Question 1：

According to the passage, what are the first computers?

（考生 A 和 B 同时回答，时间 20 秒）

Question 2：

What do you usually do on computer?

（考生 A 和 B 同时回答，时间 20 秒）

高分秘诀

（1）第一问根据短文内容作答，"早期的计算机有哪些？"答题时需要注意"first computers"这一关键词。

（2）第二问根据短文主题"计算机"作答，问考生在日常生活中都用计算机做什么。在计算机全面普及的今天，该问题非常容易作答，考生简要说明计算机在自己日常生活中的功能或作用即可。

参考答案

Question 1：

One kind of the first computers is located in Great Britain. It is a man-made circle of large stones. People used it to measure the weather and predict the change of seasons. Another ancient computer is the abacus. The early Chinese, Romans, Greeks, and Egyptians used this device to count and calculate.

最早的计算机之一在大不列颠，这是一个人造的大石头群。人们用它来测量天气和预测季节的变化。另外一个古老的计算机是算盘。早期的中国人、罗马人、希腊人和埃及人使用这个装置来计数和计算。

Question 2：

Computers are useful in many ways. Firstly, I can learn the latest news by surfing the Internet. Secondly, I can store a large amount of useful information on my computer. Besides, it is convenient for me to finish my assignments on computers because of their powerful functions.

计算机在许多方面都是有用的。首先，我可以通过上网了解最新的新闻。其次，我可以在计算机上储存大量有用的信息。此外，由于计算机功能强大，对我来说，在计算机上完成作业非常方便。

精彩表达

latest news 最新消息

a large amount of 大量（后跟不可数名词）

assignment 作业；分配

function 功能；宴会；函数

（四）Task 3　Individual Presentation

In this task, you are to talk about the picture displayed on the screen. You will have 45 seconds to prepare and 1 minute to talk about it. Now here is the picture.

A Shameful Business

（考生准备时间 45 秒）

Now please start speaking on hearing the beep.

（考生 A 和 B 同时回答，时间 1 分钟）

高分秘诀

第一步：描述图片内容。图片讲了有些人通过网络找写手完成一些工作或学习任务，如总结、论文、报告和演讲稿等。

第二步：分析图片想要揭示的内容。从网上找人代写来应付工作、学习任务，这种社会现象催生了网上非法交易。

第三步：表达自己的观点或做出评价，指出问题的严重性。

参考答案

From the picture, we can see/ that anything can happen online nowadays. When you have a report to compose, when you have a speech to prepare, when you have a summary to write, or when you have a paper to finish, you can access those guys online, whom you pay to do those jobs. There is a market, believe it or not, in which people can get every task done online. It's a shameful business.

Those guys hired online/ intend to make money from those people, who are unwilling/ to bother figuring out/ and completing their written assignments/ on their own. It is undeniable/that such writing is very likely patched together/ from other copyrighted writings. So those online "writers" violate the law. They earn money illegally.

Meanwhile I'd say it's a shame/ that some people are losing their initiative. They are unwilling/ to take pains/ in learning and training. If the situation were to continue, they would pay a high price in the long run.

从图片中，我们可以看到，如今任何事情都可能在网上发生。当你要撰写一个报告，当你需要准备一个演讲，当你要完成一个总结，或当你需要完成一篇论文时，你可以从网上联系这些人，只要付给他们相应的酬金，他们就会帮你做上述工作。不管你信不信，这是一个市场，人们可以在网上让别人完成每一项任务。这是一种可耻的交易。

那些网络代写想从不愿意自己动手完成书面任务的人那里赚钱。不可否认，这样的写作很可能是将其他有版权的著作拼凑在一起。所以网上的那些"写手"违反了法律。他们是在非法牟利。

另外，遗憾的是，有些人正在逐渐失去学习的主动性。他们不愿意下功夫学习和实践。如果这种情形继续下去，从长远来看，他们会为此付出惨痛的代价。

精彩表达

online 在线的

believe it or not（插入语）信不信由你

a shameful business 可耻的交易

complete one's written assignments 完成书面作业

violate the law 犯法

earn money illegally 非法赚钱

it's a shame 遗憾的是……

lose one's initiative 失去主动性；失去主动权

take pains 下功夫，努力

（五）Task 4　Pair Work

In this task, you are to talk with your partner about computer use in daily life. Suppose you want to exchange ideas of computer use in daily life with your partner. Talk with each other. Your talk may include：

（1）what roles computer plays in daily life

（2）what advantages of computers are

（3）what disadvantages of computers are

You will have 1 minute to prepare and three minutes to talk. Remember, this is a pair activity and you need to interact with each other. Your performance will be judged according to your contribution to the pair work. Now please start to prepare.

（屏幕显示以下文字）

（1）what roles computer plays in daily life

（2）what advantages of computers are

（3）what disadvantages of computers are

（考生准备时间 1 分钟）

Now please start your talk on hearing the beep.

（考生 A 和 B 讨论，时间 3 分钟）

Thank you. That is the end of the test.

答题要点

由题目说明可知，对话的主题是谈论计算机，对话内容包括三个方面：计算机的作用、计算机的优点及计算机的缺点。结合自己的经历回答即可,注意采用"反馈+新话题"的对话模式,即在对话中主动进行话题转换,保持对话顺畅进行。

参考答案

A: Well, let's begin our talk! We all know computers have become an indispensable part in our life. Do you think computers have changed your life in any way?

嗯,我们开始对话吧!众所周知,计算机已经成为我们生活中必不可少的一部分。计算机是否在某些方面改变了你的生活?

B: Yes, absolutely. I think computers have made enormous changes in my life. It seems that we cannot live in the modern world without them. As a matter of fact, they facilitate different aspects of my life, such as working style and forms of entertainment.

肯定是的。我认为计算机极大地改变了我的生活。在现代社会,没有计算机我们好像就无法生活。事实上,计算机能让我生活的各个方面变得便利,比如工作方式和娱乐方式。

A: What do you mean by working style and forms of entertainment?

你所说的工作方式和娱乐方式是指什么?

B: For example, I can type words, figures or data through the keyboard of my computer, which, I think, is more efficient compared with handwriting. What's more, computers have enriched my recreational activities and I can play video games or go shopping online.

例如,我可以通过计算机键盘键入单词、数字或数据,我认为这样比手写效率更高。更重要的是,计算机丰富了我的娱乐活动,我可以玩视频游戏或网购。

A: Yes. You sure can. However, I just try not to use computers very much in my life, because it seems there are many disadvantages. For instance, sitting in front of the computer for a long time is harmful for my eyesight and physical health. Also, I feel headache when I stare at the monitor over 30 minutes.

是的,你当然可以这样。然而,我在生活中会尽量避免过多地使用计算机,因为过多使用计算机会带来很多负面影响。例如,在计算机前久坐会对我的视力和身体健康有害。此外，我盯着显示器超过 30 分钟就会感到头痛。

B：Yes, sitting in front of the screen for a long time has a detrimental influence on people's health, and a sedentary lifestyle can cause some chronic diseases, like headache or stuff like that. My suggestion is that you just keep working out, playing badminton, swimming and so on, then the bad influence can be minimized. Anyway, computers are useful in everyday life.

是的，长时间坐在屏幕前会对人的健康产生不利影响，久坐的生活方式会导致一些慢性疾病，如头痛或类似的问题。我的建议是，你只要坚持锻炼，如打羽毛球、游泳等，就可以最大限度地减少计算机带来的负面影响。无论如何，计算机在日常生活中还是很有用的。

A：You bet. It is necessary in my life too. I use it to connect to the Internet, communicate with friends through some instant messaging programs, browse the web, download music and save them to my removable hard drive... It is a daily necessity.

当然，计算机在我的生活中也是必不可少的。我用它来上网，通过一些即时通信软件与朋友沟通，浏览网页，下载音乐并保存到我的可移动硬盘……计算机是日常必需品。

精彩表达

as a matter of fact 事实上

facilitate different aspects of my life 使我生活的各个方面变得便利

recreational activities 娱乐活动

第二章 英语阅读学习策略与指导

在阅读过程中，借助上下文、文章结构或背景知识等线索理解词语、段落或全文的意思称为阅读策略。比如，借助上下文线索推测词义、根据篇章结构线索迅速捕捉文章大意等。本章主要介绍了阅读技巧解读、阅读教学与评价、阅读训练三部分内容。

第一节 阅读技巧解读

一、略读技巧

（一）略读的基本技巧

不同的阅读材料用不同的阅读速度。阅读轻松休闲的小说类读物时，通常速度较快；阅读非小说类的读物，或完成作业时，情况就不同了，读科研报告需要高度集中精力才行。然而，有时为了节省时间，也得用快读法来阅读非小说类的读物。

这里需要掌握的就是"浏览法"和"查阅法"这两种阅读技巧，这两种方法都是快速而有选择地略读的技巧。

1. 查阅

"查阅法"是为了获取某一具体、特定信息而采取的快速阅读技巧，也可解释为搜寻式阅读。它是一种从阅读材料中有目的、有选择地迅速查找某一具体事实或特定信息的技能，要求快速、准确。查阅词典、百科全书、索引、人物传记、科普文章等都需要熟练的查阅技巧。查阅时先看问题，弄清所要查找的是什么信息，如数字、日期、姓名等，然后在文章中查阅，一看到相关部分就细读，读者在找到了他所需要的确切信息之后就完成了阅读任务，没有必要逐字逐句地阅读理解。

怎样进行"查阅法"阅读呢？在开始阅读前应了解其编排形式，然后进行查阅。任何资料都是按照某种逻辑方式排列的。如词典、百科全书、索引按照字母顺序排列，节目单、体育比赛、历史资料按时间顺序排列，体育节目还可按照类别排列等。对于图表、报刊广告、说明书、时间表、菜单等则应认真阅读其中不同的缩写和符号，迅速找到所需信息。

（1）依据阅读文本中提供的各种线索

①大写字母

专有名词的首字母大写，如人名、地名、国名、书名等。另外，缩略语的字母要大写，如 U.N.（联合国）等。大写字母比较醒目，在文章中容易查找。

②阿拉伯数字

文章中的阿拉伯数字，如年份、日期等，也很醒目，便于迅速查询。

③目录、标题、索引

在日常学习、工作生活中，经常要查阅一些资料。比如，我们想了解全球空气污染的状况或想以此为主题写一篇文章，这时需要查阅有关参考书。找到参考书后，借助书中目录以及各章节中的大小标题可以较快地查询到有关空气污染的信息。如果是英文学术著作，查询书结尾附录中的索引（Glossary 或 Index）十分方便。通常附录中包括两种索引，一种按书中提及的学者姓名编排，一种按讨论的主题编排。

④栏目、图片

在报刊上查询信息可以借助栏目、图片等。比如，读者要读体育新闻，应查找体育版块或体育栏目，要看汽车行情，可翻阅查找带汽车图片的广告。

（2）查阅工具书

查询资料通常要使用各种工具书，包括纸质工具书和电子（如光盘等）工具书，比如英英、英汉、汉英词典、百科全书等。工具书，尤其是电子工具书，信息量大，种类齐全，涉及各类学科。工具书中列有详细的分类目录，正文中的条目按英文字母或汉语拼音顺序编排，因此查阅资料很方便。通常，电子工具书不仅提供目录索引，而且还配有搜索引擎，查询资料更加便利快捷。

（3）上网查询

①利用搜索引擎

利用互联网查询资料简单、快速而方便。查找资料要使用搜索引擎，常用的搜索引擎有百度、谷歌等。

②如何输入关键词

A. 输入英文关键词查英文资料

在网上查询英文资料简单、方便，利用搜索引擎查找所需英文资料即可。比如，想查一下美国篮球运动员乔丹是哪一年出生的，可以按以下步骤查询：

a. 输入关键词

输入英文单词："Jordan NBA birthday"，注意单词间要有空格。

b. 查看搜索结果

结果显示乔丹是1963年出生的。

c. 分析搜索结果

要判断以上搜索结果是否可靠真实。

d. 输入不同的关键词核对搜索结果

输入英文单词："Michael Jordan NBA birth"。

Michael Jordan biography bio- ［翻译此页 BETA］

Michael Jeffrey Jordan was born on February 17, 1963, in Brooklyn, New York, but his family decided to move to... The team had such college players as Jordan, Patrick Ewing, Chris Mullin.

B. 输入中文关键词查中文资料

步骤同上（输入英文关键词查英文资料）。

C. 输入英文关键词查中文资料

想要知道一英文词语，如"Gone with the Wind"的中文意思，可以使用搜索引擎搜索。

a. 输入中英文关键词

输入"Gone with the Wind 风"。注意一定要输入一个与英文词相关的汉字或词组，否则查询结果仅显示英文。

b. 查看搜索结果

虽然有搜索结果，但无法断定该词语的中文意思。

c. 重新输入英文关键词，更换中文关键词

如果我们知道该词语是电影名，可输入"Gone with the Wind 电影"；如果知道该词语是小说名，可输入"Gone with the Wind 小说"，然后进行搜索。

d. 查看搜索结果

上一段讲的两种关键词输入法都可以搜索到该词语的中文意思:《飘》或《乱世佳人》两种译法。

（4）利用校园网内部资源查询

一般高校图书馆都有大量的电子资源，电子资源包括"中国学术会议全文数据库"和其他各种数据库，仅国内外学术期刊就有上万种。电子资源都有简单便利的检索系统，利用这种资源进行学习研究，方便、省时、效率高。

2. 浏览

"浏览"是为了获得对某一读物的总体印象而采取的快速阅读技巧。比如，想知道电影值不值得看，于是去浏览一下简介，也就是"预先看"的意思。对于一部长篇小说，预先看一下人物、背景、主要章节，然后决定是否阅读全篇；对于非小说类的读物，同样可以预先看一看作者讨论的是什么话题、观点是什么、文章中是否有足够的论据等。

怎样进行"浏览法"略读呢？

第一，先看文章的标题及所有的小标题。

第二，把第一段稍微仔细地看一下，它通常是引入话题的段落。

第三，再看每一个段落的主题句（大部分是第一句或最后一句）。

第四，对标有数字的句子重点看一下。

第五，阅读最后的总结句，或总结段，或总结部分。

(二)略读技巧策略解析

1.Reading 1

After the violent earthquake that shook Los Angeles in 1994, earthquake scientists had good news to report: The damage and death toll(死亡人数)could have been much worse.

More than 60 people died in this earthquake. By comparison, an earthquake of similar intensity that shook America in 1988 claimed 25 000 victims.

Injuries and deaths were relatively less in Los Angeles because the quake occurred at 4:31 a.m. On a holiday, when traffic was light on the city's highways. In addition, changes made to the construction codes in Los Angeles during the last 20 years have strengthened the city's buildings and highways, making them more resistant to quakes.

Despite the good news, civil engineers aren't resting on their successes. Pinned to their drawing boards are blueprints(蓝图)for improved quake-resistant buildings. The new designs should offer even greater security to cities where earthquakes often take place.

In the past, making structures quake-resistant meant firm yet flexible materials, such as steel and wood, that bend without breaking. Later, people tried to lift a building of its foundation, and insert rubber and steel between the building and its foundation to reduce the impact of ground vibrations. The most recent designs give buildings brains as well as concrete and steel supports. Called smart buildings, the structures respond like living organisms to an earthquake's vibrations. When the ground shakes and the building tips forward, the computer would force the building to shift in the opposite direction.

The new smart structures could be very expensive to build. However, they would save many lives and would be less likely to be damaged during earthquakes.

1. One reason why the loss of lives in the Los Angeles earthquake was comparatively low is that ____.

A. new computers had been installed in the building

B. it occurred in the residential areas rather than on the highway

C. large numbers of Los Angeles residents had gone for a holiday

D. improvements had been made in the construction of buildings and highways

2. The function of the computer mentioned in the passage is to ____.

A. counterbalance an earthquake's action on the building

B. predict the coming of an earthquake with accuracy

C. help strengthen the foundation of the building

D. measure the impact of an earthquake's vibrations

3. The smart buildings discussed in the passage ____.

A. would cause serious financial problems

B. would be worthwhile though costly

C. would increase the complexity of architectural design

D. can reduce the ground vibrations caused by earthquakes

4. It can be inferred from the passage that in minimizing the damage caused by earthquakes attention should be focused on ____.

A. the increasing use of rubber and steel in capital construction

B. the development of flexible building materials

C. the reduction of the impact of ground vibrations

D. early forecasts of earthquakes

5. The author's main purpose in writing the passage is to ____.

A. compare the consequences of the earthquakes that occurred in the U.S.

B. encourage civil engineers to make more extensive use of computers

C. outline the history of the development of quake-resistant building materials

D. report new developments in constructing quake resistant buildings

这是一篇关于房屋建筑与抗震的文章。我们用"浏览"的快读方法把每一段的第一句看一下。文章第一段以洛杉矶大地震引出话题；第二段说对比之下伤亡较小；第三段说明原因，其中之一是建筑物从设计方面采取了革新的措施；第四段说工程师还在努力设计出抗震的房屋；第五段说以前注重房屋材料的改进，过渡到现在有房屋结构上安装电脑的设想；最后一段说这种新结构的好处。这样整篇文章就把握住了，然后用"查阅法"去做以下的题目：

1. D 项是正确答案。这是一道细节题，依据在第三段第二句 because 后面的意思可以得出正确的理解。文中提到建筑法规定必须对建筑物及公路进行抗震改进。

B 项不对。相反，这可能是伤亡严重的原因。

C 项不对。那天是休假日，并非大家都已离家去度假。

A 项不对。装有电脑的大楼是文章中提到的最新设计，洛杉矶地震时还没有。

2. A 项是正确答案。这是一道细节题，依据在第五段最后一句。文中提到智能型的建筑物装有电脑，在房屋倾斜时，指挥它朝相反方向平衡。Counter 是一个前缀，是"相反的，对着的"的意思。

B 项不对。电脑在此的用途并非精确预报地震。

C 项不对。现在的新方法不在于加固地基，犯了"想当然"的错误。

D 项不对。电脑的作用也不是用来测定振幅。

3. B 项是正确答案。这是一道细节题，依据在最后一段。文中提到 very expensive，但转折词 however 告诉我们，因能拯救宝贵的生命，花昂贵的钱是值得的。

A 项不对。"会引起财政问题"，言下之意不会采用，与文章的意思不符。

C 项不对。"增加设计难度"，文中没有提到。

D 项不对。以前用填充材料来"减少地基的震动"，现在讨论的是新设计的装有电脑的建筑，当房屋倾斜时，起反方向平衡作用。犯了搜寻细节不准确的毛病。

4. C 项是正确答案。这是一道推论题，依据在第五段。新思路的目的是减少对地基的冲击力。

A 项不对。填充橡胶及钢筋材料是过去的办法。

B 项不对。用伸缩性材料也是过去的办法。

D 项不对。提早预报能减少损失，但本文没有讨论这个问题。

5. D 项是正确答案。这是一道有关中心思想的题目。本文描述为了抗震，建筑物从设计、材料以及结构诸方面进行革新的措施。

A项不对。开头把洛杉矶地震与其他地震相比，为了引出本文的话题。

B项不对。最新设计中有电脑控制的建筑物，但中心思想不是鼓励工程师使用电脑、在哪方面使用，偷换了概念。

C项不对。文中提到建筑材料的改进，并非讨论建筑材料的历史，把中心思想归纳成抗震材料的发展史，显然不对。

2. Reading 2

Our Dreams

Let us begin by saying what does not cause our dreams. Our dreams do not come from "another world". They are not messages from some outside source. They are not a look into the future, either.

All our dreams have something to do with our emotions, fears, longings, wishes, needs and memories. But something on the "outside" may affect what we dream. If a person is hungry, or tired, or cold, his dreams may include a feeling of this kind. If the covers on your body, such as a quilt or a blanket, have slipped off your bed, you may dream that you are sleeping or resting on the ice and snow. The material for the dream you will have tonight is likely to come from the experiences you have today.

So the subject of your dream usually comes from something that has effect on you while you are sleeping (feeling of cold, a noise, a discomfort, etc.) and it may also use your past experiences and the wishes and interests you have now. This is why very young children are likely to dream of fairies, older children of examinations, hungry people of food, homesick soldiers of their families, and prisoners of freedom.

To show you how that is happening while you are asleep and how your wishes or needs can all be joined together in a dream, here is the story of an experiment. A man was asleep and the back of his hand was rubbed with a piece of absorbent cotton. He would dream that he was in a hospital and his charming girl friend was visiting him, sitting on the bed and feeling gently his hand!

There are some scientists who have made a special study of why we dream, what we dream and what those dreams mean. Their explanation of dreams, though a bit reasonable, is not accepted by everyone, but it offers an interesting approach to the problem. They believe that dreams are mostly expressions of wishes that did not come true. In other words, a dream is a way of having your wishes carried out.

1. According to the author, our dreams ____.

A. are simply messages from another world

B. have little connection with our emotions, wishes or needs

C. are a curious look into the future

D. are to some degree caused by some of our feelings

2. If the covers have slipped off your bed, you may dream that ____.

A. something comfortable happens to you

B. some people are making noise

C. you are staying in freezing surroundings

D. you have nothing on at all

3. When the back of a man's hand was rubbed with a piece of absorbent cotton in the experiment, he would dream that ____.

A. his hand was being struck by someone

B. his hand was badly hurt by something

C. his hand was gently touched by his sweetheart

D. somebody was wiping sweat off his body

4. When a person feels hungry, he is likely to dream of ____.

A. wonderful fairies

B. fine food and drinks

C. lovely young girls

D. his family members

5. Some scientists' explanation of dreams ____.

A. does not give an outlet for our wishes

B. offers a meaningful approach to the problem

C. gives us an exact answer to the problem

D. is widely accepted and thought highly of by the public

答案：1. D   2. C   3. C   4. B   5. B

注释：

[第1题] 使用策略：标题；略读；主题句；首尾段

答案为 D（are to some degree caused by some of our feelings）。此题问文章大意（main idea）。读文章标题时，我们了解到本文谈论的是"梦"，但所获信息较笼统，回答此题需要获得进一步的信息。略读每段找出各段主题句，发现该段主题句在第 2 段第 1 句：All our dreams have something to do with our emotions, fears, longings, wishes, needs and memories，意为"我们所做的梦与我们的情绪、恐惧、渴望、意愿、需求及记忆有关"，是答案 D 的主要依据，该主题也是本篇的中心思想。读本文末段进一步确认第 2 段主题是本文的主题，故选 D。

二、掌握中心思想

（一）领会中心思想

在阅读理解过程中，掌握中心思想是一项非常重要的技能。只有掌握了中心思想，我们才能进行有效的阅读。提高阅读理解能力的第一步（即关键的一步）就是掌握文章的中心思想。看完文章之后，应该问一下自己：文章到底说了些什么？这有助于读者把握全局，而不是盯着零碎的细节死啃。要弄明白一篇文章的中心思想，还应该先弄明白每个段落的中心思想，因为一篇文章是由几个段落组成的。如果能找出每个段落的中心，同样能找出一篇短文的中心，一个章节的中心，乃至一整本书的中心。

通常一个段落是意思相互关联的一个整体，表达一个意思。因此可以通过找段落的中心句来确定段落的中心思想。一个段落的中心往往以主题句的形式表示，一篇文章的中心就以它的主题段落来表示。70%～90% 的主题句出现在段落的开头，对有关话题先作总的陈述，然后细讲，即"先总后分"的模式。主题句也可能出现在段落的末尾，对前面的具体陈述作一个概括，即"先分后总"的模式。主题句也会出现在段落的中间，这时它起桥梁的作用，连接前后的陈述，即"由分到总"，又"由总到分"的模式。有时段首提出了中心句，段末再概括一下，即起到强调作用，又起到呼应作用。

为了形象地理解段落的主题句和其他句子之间的关系，我们来打个比方。我们打开一把伞，伞面覆盖了所有的骨架，而所有的骨架支撑着伞面。我们可以把伞面比作中心思想，把伞的骨架比作具体细节。伞面好比是作者想要表达的观点，一个很概括的陈述；骨架则是作者用来解释，或者证明，或者支持这一陈述的具体内容。

（二）难点分析

Passage 1

Norms serve the function of standardizing behavior , of bringing order to what otherwise would be a chaotic situation. If some of us drove on the left side of the road and others on the right side, or if some of us stopped for red lights while others did not, there would be much confusion and danger. In other words , social life as we know it would not be possible without norms. All cultures have a system of norms to provide such social control for a society.

The author's primary purpose in this passage is to ____.

A. explain the function of norms for social control

B. refute the belief that norms are unimportant

C. instruct readers about which norms are appropriate in some cultures

D. establish social norms that are especially popular in the United States

在阅读这一小段前，可先浏览一下问题选项。了解"作者写这一段的目的"，大致归纳中心思想，然后带着问题去阅读。一边阅读，一边思考作者到底想告诉我们什么。阅读时不宜慌张，以自己的正常速度仔细阅读。把一些重要信息、关键词划出来，这些划出来的信息、关键词应该始终与读者思考着的问题有关。

目前流行的阅读理解题是多项选择题，即要求选出最佳答案。因此得逐项分析，排除那些无关的、矛盾的、不合理的选项。

上面段落后面的问题是检查读者对中心思想的理解。第一句是主题句，选项 A 的表述与主题句很接近，可能是答案。在这种情况下，有些人后面的选项看都不去看了，马上选 A，这种方法不可取，还是要仔细读完各个选项，然后再作选择。另外，解此题时，要研究每个选项的第一个动词。B 项 "refute（驳斥）" 这个词与文章的整体印象不符，应排除。C 项 "instruct（告知）" 与文中的信息无关。D 项 "establish（建立）" 虽然与文章不是完全无关，提到要建立标准制度，但没有特别提到过美国。因此 A 项是最佳选择，"explain（解释）" 标准对社会控制所起的作用。

Passage 2

Osiris, Egyptian god of the underworld, was often portrayed in mummy wrappings. Isis, frequently represented with a cow's head or horns, was a nature goddess. Ra was the sun god whose symbol was the pyramid. Amon was often represented as a ram or with a ram's head.

Which is the implied main idea?

A. The most important Egyptian god was Ra.

B. Egyptian religious is interesting.

C. Egyptian gods were drawn as animals.

D. The Egyptians had several gods.

这一小段没有主题句，因此需要做出归纳。A 项是支持中心思想的具体细节，而不是中心思想。B 项的外延太大，即归纳得太广、太笼统。C 项是不正确的，因为文中只提到两个神被画成动物，不是所有的神，此句也不能暗示本段的中心思想。因此 D 项能概括本段，是本段的中心表述。

三、语篇阅读

良好的阅读习惯，不仅会提高阅读速度，而且会提高理解的准确率。为了培养良好的阅读习惯，要克服一些不良的阅读习惯，如指读、摇头读、默读或出声读、回读和译读等。要逐步养成按意群阅读和在语篇层面上阅读的习惯，并准确把握句子与句子之间、段落与段落之间的逻辑关系。

（一）了解句子基础功能

一个表意清楚、结构完整且过渡自然的有效段落，必须要有且仅有一个明确的中心思想（central idea 或者 theme）。而为了突显这个中心思想，作者常常在段落的开头、中间或末尾安排一个主题句（topic sentence），并对其进行恰当的拓展（development），还在句子与句子之间进行恰当的衔接，形成过渡自然（smooth transition）的效果。

从以上分析我们可以看出组成段落的句子主要有三种：主题句、拓展句（developing sentence）和结论句（concluding sentence）。因而，段落的基本结构可用下列数学等式表示：

段落 = 主题句 + 拓展句 + 拓展句 + 拓展句……+ 结论句

1. 主题句

主题句是高度概括段落主题思想的句子，用来介绍段落的中心话题或者主要内容。主题句在一个自然段中起核心作用，它告诉我们本段的主要内容。因而，主题句是一个段落最重要的句子，是整段文章的"灵魂和统帅"，段落中其他的所有句子都必须围绕它而展开。

主题句在段落中的位置是比较灵活的，可以放在段首，可以在段落中间，也可出现在段尾，有时在首句和尾句中同时出现，十分醒目。在有的段落中，主题句甚至不直接出现，而是隐藏在字里行间，需要细细体会。

2. 拓展句

拓展句是对主题句的展开说明、论证，是以具体的细节对主题思想进行阐述、论证、说明、引申和补充，用来进一步说明或者支持主题句，使之更充实、明晰。

3. 结论句

结论句是对这一段内容的概括和总结。通常，结论句就是用另一种词组、句型、表达方法来再现主题。好的结论句一方面可以和主题句相呼应，对主题思想做进一步的深化；另一方面，可以显示结构的完整性。

在结论句中使用的连接词主要有 in brief、in conclusion、in short、in sum、in summary、to sum up、to summarize、to conclude、all in all 等。

4. 论点陈述句

在篇章中，作者往往需要若干段落来阐述自己的观点，因此在整个篇章中找到作者的论点（thesis statement）是关键。在多数情况下，论点在第一个段落，或者前面的几个段落中出现，而后面的段落往往是说明、支持论点的，并且每个段落又有自己的主题句。例如：

America is experiencing a health care crisis because of an aging population and rising health care costs.

The North won the American civil war because of its larger population and stronger industrial base, which allowed it to make more weapons and supplies than the South.

了解了句子在段落中的功能，我们就能提高阅读速度，并更准确地理解文章大意。

（二）理解句子与句子之间的逻辑关系

除了要了解句子在段落中的功能之外，还应该对段落中句子与句子之间的起承转合关系一目了然，这样就知道什么时候可以略而不读，什么时候要放慢速度，什么时候要引起注意。比如说，如果我们只想了解文章的大意，看到作者在第一句提出自己的观点之后，用了"for example"这个提示词，那么这个例子不管有多长，我们都可以一扫而过，不必细读，因为这个例子只是对作者观点的例证。但是如果出现 however、but 这样的提示词，我们就要放慢速度了，看看作者是否提出不同的或者新的观点。如果见到 on the whole 之类的词，就知道作者要总结了，这也是值得注意的地方。

表 2-1-1 所列举的是英语中常见的连接词及其功能。

表 2-1-1　英语中常见的连接词及功能

功能	举例
顺序	first, firstly, second, secondly, to begin with, then, after, before, next, formerly, afterwards, simultaneously
举例	for example, for instance, such as, similarly, to illustrate, namely, to demonstrate, take...as an example, a case in point is..., ...serves as an example

续表

功能	举例
列举	at last, besides, first, first of all, firstly, finally, in the first place, to begin with, to start with, second, secondly, what is more, furthermore, in addition, in addition to, moreover, last but not least
比较	also, as, as...as, at the same time, both, compared with, each, like, likewise, similarly, the same as
对比	although, but, however, in contrast with/to, instead of, nevertheless, on the contrary, on the other hand, the opposite, unlike, while, whereas, yet
总结	as a result, finally, in a word, therefore, in brief, in short, in summary, thus, consequently, accordingly, in conclusion, so, on the whole, lastly, to sum up
转折	though, although, yet, despite, nevertheless, in spite of, despite, however, but, otherwise, on the contrary, in contrast, whereas, alternatively
递进	and, likewise, I besides, also, in addition, furthermore, as well as, moreover, what is more
因果	as, as a result of, account for, because, because of, consequently, considering that, due to, for, lead to, now that, on the ground of, owing to, result in, seeing that, since, so, thanks to, then, therefore, the reason why

当然，很多连接词不仅仅只有一种功能，在具体的上下文中可以很清楚地理解该词的特定意义和功能。连接词就像交通路口的红绿灯一样，给我们明确的提示，要求我们迅速做出反应，因此连接词对我们了解作者的观点态度和篇章布局非常重要。

（三）掌握段落和篇章的布局

英文中段落和篇章的布局（paragraph patterns）方式主要有：顺序法、举例说明法、分类法、定义解释法、概括法、比较法、列举法、类比法（或叫模拟法）、因果关系法。从它们的名称上我们可以清楚地看出它们各自的特点。在大多数情况下，作者往往不会只采用一种布局方式，而是灵活地将几种方式组合起来，因此就有了混合法这种新的谋篇布局的方式。

1. 顺序法

顺序法在记叙文和说明文中常常用到。当作者要叙述一件事情发生的过程、一个程序的操作步骤时，使用顺序法可以使结构清晰。常用的顺序法有时间顺序法、空间顺序法、主次顺序法、步骤顺序法和发展变化顺序法。

（1）时间顺序法（Development by time）

作者在讲故事和叙述事件经过时，最简单、最直接的方法就是按时间顺序进行：先发生的事情先讲，后发生的事情后讲。

（2）空间顺序法（Development by space）

空间，有大有小，可大到整个地球乃至整个宇宙，也可以小至一个房间乃至一个书桌的抽屉。空间顺序法，主要用于描述一个空间及其中各细节之间在位置或者方位上的相互关系。作者在描写空间时，无论其大小，必然会先确定一个方位，并以此为参照点，按照从上到下或从下到上、从远到近或从近到远、从左到右或从右到左、由内到外或由外到内，或者按照顺时针方向或逆时针方向叙述，而且作者在叙述过程中不能也不会在中途变换参照点。

（3）主次顺序法（Development by importance）

主次顺序法是指作者在材料的组织安排过程中，按重要性程度递减或递增的顺序来排列。可以将最为重要的信息排在最前面，依次递减；也可以反过来，将最次要的信息放在最前面，依次递增，这种方法较多使用在议论文中。

（4）步骤顺序法（Development by process）

当要讲解如何做某事或完成某项任务时，作者通常采用步骤顺序法，进行逐步叙述。当然，在使用步骤顺序法进行写作时，作者一定会尊重客观事实，不会有任何的主观渲染，会在整个叙述过程中按照事件发展的本来过程描述，不会有跳跃。

（5）发展变化顺序法（Development by change）

顾名思义，发展变化顺序法就是按照事物本身发展变化的过程来对事物进行说明。当然，任何事物的发展变化都少不了与时间有关。与时间顺序法不同的是，在按照发展变化顺序法写作时，文章并不一定要把时间交代得非常具体。

2. 举例说明法

举例说明法，也叫例证法，是最常用也是最有效的方法之一。作者用自己的亲身经历或他人的事例来具体地说明或证实中心思想。举例说明法通常使用一个主题句，直截了当地阐述自己的观点，然后运用一些具体事例来对其进行具体介绍、说明、证实或解释。

3. 分类法

分类法就是按照事物的某种特质，如大小、颜色、质地、来源、所在位置、用途等，将其归并成若干类别或范畴。

4. 定义解释法

有时候，作者在写作时为了防止读者混淆或产生误解，要把多数读者不熟悉的词、术语或概念进行解释或下定义。下定义就是对所谈论的事物给出一个科学的说明，解释是说话者根据自己对事物的理解给出一个客观的说明。

5. 概括法

概括法就是对某一事物进行总体说明，在文中形成一个主题句，并用一些具体事例来进行论证。概括法通常有"总—分""分—总""总—分—总"三种模式。

6. 比较法

为了帮助人们对一个不太熟悉的事物获得一个清晰的认识和了解，作者常常拿一个人们比较熟悉的事物与之放在一起进行对照，找出这两个事物之间的相同点或相似性，这就是比较。运用比较法进行写作是一种常见的段落拓展方法，在运用比较法写作时，作者通常采用两种模式：平行比较（parallel comparison）和完全比较（complete comparison）。

平行比较，就是以事物的相似点为线索，同时对双方进行逐一对应的比较，其具体模式为 Point 1：Subject A，Subject B；Point 2：Subject A，Subject B；Point 3：Subject A，Subject... 完全比较，就是以事物本身为线索，先对一个事物的各方面进行全面叙述，再把另一事物的各方面与该事物相对应地进行全面叙述，其具体模式为 Subject A：Point 1，Point 2，Point 3...Subject B：Point 1，Point 2，Point 3...

7. 列举法

列举法在叙述文、说明文和议论文的写作中都十分实用。使用列举法可以使文章层次清晰，思路明确，论证有力。

8. 类比法

类比法或模拟法是一种特殊的比较法，其具体方法就是借助于一个大家熟知的事物说明另一个我们不了解的且与其不同类的事物，也就是要在两个不同类型的事物之间找出相似点，以便我们准确理解较难理解的事物。

9. 因果关系法

因果关系法就是根据事件发生的原因和结果之间的逻辑关系拓展段落。这种方法反映了人们如何根据事件的原因分析其结果或根据事件的结果推断其原因。与此相对应，运用因果关系法通常有两种模式：先因后果或先果后因。当然，作者在进行因果关系推理时，一定会注意逻辑关系的严谨性，尊重客观事实，避免把偶然当必然，当然也不能省略因果链上的任何环节。以下是两个最基本的逻辑关系：

充分条件：有之必然，无之未必不然。

必要条件：无之必不然，有之未必然。

四、过渡词

（一）留意过渡词

过渡词是连接句子的不同部分、连接两个或者更多的句子，连接文章表达的两个或者更多不同思想的转换词。

就像在公路上驾车行驶，路上的路标、路牌不断告诉前面哪里有急转弯，有陡坡，前面十字路口是什么路，过渡词让我们知道作者写了些什么内容，作者的想法，作者在什么地方转换了话题或观点。作者通过使用不同的过渡词，构成了不同的表达模式，使意群与意群之间、句子与句子之间、段落与段落之间、章节与章节之间得以完美地衔接与过渡。过渡词还有一个重要的作用，那就是有助于区分什么是重要细节，什么是非重要细节，什么是第一层次的细节，什么是第二层次的细节，这样就能更好地厘清文章的脉络，把握文章的中心。

在通常情况下，作者会以一定的模式来组织文章，如描写关系、空间关系、过程关系、顺序关系、举例关系、分类关系、因果关系、比较与对比关系、类比关系、定义关系等。其实每种模式都有不同的"过渡词"，一旦能训练自己辨认出作者使用的"过渡词",就会很容易看出作者的组织模式,也就能更好地理解作者所要表达的意思,理解整篇文章的中心思想。

因此在阅读时应该养成注意"过渡词"的习惯,这样有利于提高阅读理解能力。比如,在阅读中看到"and""in addition"之类的过渡词,就可放心地继续下去,因为作者下面说的东西与前面的一样,当读到"but""however"之类的过渡词时,应该知道作者要转向了,必须小心,仔细研究作者观点转到了哪里。

以下是一些常用的过渡词,如表 2-1-2 所示:

表 2-1-2　英语中常用过渡词

递增	and, moreover, plus, furthermore, in addition, again, first, second, least important, more important, most important
过程	first, second, third, next, then, finally, to begin with, in the next
空间关系	right, left, up, down, above, below, in front of, behind
转折	but, however, yet, on the other hand, though, although, nevertheless, instead, meanwhile, in the meantime, after all
类似比较	in other words, that is to say, similarly, in comparison, like, likewise, so
因果	as a result, thus, because, therefore, hence, consequently, the reason, so
举例	for example, for instance, a case in point
时间顺序	at first, later, after that, finally, once, earlier, eventually, when, now
总结	to sum up, to conclude, in sum, in conclusion, in short, in a word
并列句连词	and, but, or, for, yet, still, nor, so, otherwise, while, whereas
从句连词	when, if, where, although, so long as, since, until, before, after, because, now that, for the reason that, so that, what, which, who

(二)难点分析

Passage 1

What makes physical fitness important for children? First of all, it offers the same advantages it offers adults. For instance, among other things, it benefits the heart and blood vessels, increases the capacity of the lung, and makes the bones stronger.

Secondly, it helps children control their weight. One reason weight control is especially important is that children who are overweight will often have a problem with weight all their lives. Another benefit fitness offers is psychological strength. It relieves anxiety and tension children may feel at school. It also can be effective as a treatment for depression, more of a problem in children than many people realize. In addition to these benefits, fitness offers protection from various ailments and diseases. For example, it helps prevent heart disease and high blood pressure in children.

这段短文的话题是孩子身体健康的问题。中心思想：有不少理由说明孩子身体健康是非常重要的。first、second、another、and in addition 等是表明相同意思的递进关系的过渡词，都说明锻炼身体的好处。这些过渡词连接的是第一层次上的细节，支持全文的中心思想。作者又把每一个细节展开，那是第二层意思的细节，作者用了 for example、one reason 等过渡词。

作者提到的第一点好处：（第一层意思）锻炼身体对大人有好处，对孩子也有好处。（第二层意思）用举例法说明，如增进心脏、血管、肺部的能力，强壮骨骼。

第二点好处：（第一层意思）减少体重。（第二层意思）用因果关系表明，此举减少了以后可能一辈子都会有过胖的问题。

第三点好处：（第一层意思）增加心理承受力。（第二层意思）用举例法说明，减少焦虑、紧张及沮丧。

第四点好处：（第一层意思）增加抗病能力。（第二层意思）用举例法表明，此举可减少心脏病、高血压等疾病。

Passage 2

（1）College classrooms are full of more than just eager, young faces fresh out of high school.（2）The eighteen-year-old is still there, of course, and still eager.（3）But next to him may sit someone just 88 eager——and old enough to be his granny.（4）Granny may have always wanted to learn French, and now at last her chance has come.（5）Across the room is a thirty-year-old man who may have just spent four years in the Navy.（6）He postponed his studies, but is now going to school on the G. I. Bill.（7）Right in front of him sits a housewife who found out there is just enough time for a class or two while the kids are at school. (8) And then there is the middle-aged salesman who is back in school because he wants a new career. (9) Such variety is typical of the college campus in this decade.

(G. I. Bill means government issued Bill, 指美国政府发给军人的钱)

1. What is the main idea of the paragraph?

A. College classrooms are in a mes now.

B. The young people have no advantage in college classrooms now.

C. Many people could not afford to go to college when they were young.

D. Many people of varying ages and goals are found in college classrooms these days.

2. Which sentence is the topic sentence?

A. First.

B. Second.

C. Fifth.

D. Last.

3. Which transitional word is not used in this paragraph?

A. more than

B. next to

C. across

D. in front of

4. The supporting details are organized in some type of patterns in this paragraph. Which is the exception?

A. Space relationship.

B. Example.

C. Process.

D. Contrast.

5. According to the paragraph, which group of people (other than the eighteen-year-old) are not mentioned in college classrooms today?

A. Senior citizens.

B. Adolescents.

C. Veterans.

D. New career seekers.

这篇短文说明现在的大学课堂不再是清一色刚离开学校的高中毕业生，许多不同年龄的人，为了不同的目的来到大学课堂学习，这已经不是什么新鲜事。

1. D 项是正确答案。如上所述，本文说的是这个中心思想。

2. D 项是正确答案。文中其他的句子说的都是具体细节，最后一句是总结句，是这个段落的主题句。

3. A 项是正确答案。在文中，除了 "more than" 之外，其他过渡词都能找到。

4. C 项是正确答案。这个段落列举了不同类型的学生，运用举例的模式。作者从在一个教室里他们坐在不同的位置来讲，用了空间关系的模式。作者在提到这些不同类型的学生时，同时与18岁的高中毕业生进行比较，用了对比的模式。

5. B 项是正确答案。作者提到能成为18岁高中毕业生奶奶的学生，即年长的公民；作者也提到靠政府津贴来上大学的退伍军人，即老兵；作者还提到返回学校更新知识的推销员，即想寻求新职业生涯的人，但是没有提到青少年。

五、了解和利用冗余信息

（一）冗余信息及其表现形式

冗余信息在文本中的表现形式很多，可体现在词汇、句子和段落三个层次上。

1. 词汇层次

在词汇层次上，语言冗余性主要表现为两种形式：信息复现与信息涵盖。

（1）信息复现（Information recurrence）

信息复现是一种最常见的冗余现象，指同一语言单位重复出现，这种复现形式又分为三种情况：同义复现、近义复现和反义复现。

①信息冗余现象以同义形式复现，例如：

I will never, never forgive you.

我永远永远不会原谅你。

never 在这里以同义（同词）的形式复现来加强句子的语气。

②信息冗余现象以近义形式复现，例如：

New England has some of the most fickle, or changeable weather in the country.

新英格兰气候多变。

在这一句子中，fickle 与 changeable 是近义词，我们可以根据 changeable 推测 fickle 的意思。

③信息冗余现象以反义形式复现，例如：

Jack found the trip enthralling, even though Jemmy, his sister, thought it was boring.

Jack 认为那次旅行很迷人，而他的妹妹 Jemmy 觉得枯燥无味。

在这一句中，enthralling 与 boring 就属于反义复现，由 boring 一词可知 enthralling 的意思。

这种冗余现象常用的引导词有 although、but、yet、even though、however、instead of、on the contrary、on the other hand、rather than、whereas、while 等。

我们在阅读过程中依据上下文，有效地利用冗余信息的同义、近义和反义复现，就能推测出一些生疏难懂词汇的意思，提高阅读理解能力。

（2）信息涵盖（Information cover）

信息涵盖是指一个表达单位所负载的信息包含了另一个表达单位所负载的信息。例如：

Amphibians, such as frogs and snakes, are cold-blooded.

在此句中，amphibian（水陆两栖动物）已包含了 frogs and snakes 的信息，但其所指的范围要宽得多。

这种冗余现象常用的引导词有 for example、for instance、other、such as 等。

2. 句子层次

在句子层次上，作者为了确保文中传递的信息能被读者完全理解并留下深刻的印象，使新信息得到加强，往往在下文中再重复地讲一遍，从而使第一句的内容更清楚具体，保证读者能够准确理解。例如：

Make no mistake about it, boxing is the only sport to confess injuries. It is the only pastime in which the entire object is to deliver such punishment to the opponent's brain that he is knocked out. The head is the number one target.

译文：毫无疑问，拳击是唯一被承认会引起伤害的一项运动。这种运动的全部目的在于给对手的大脑以沉重打击，从而将他打昏过去。对手的头部是首要目标。

全段共有三句。第二句部分地重复第一句的内容，目的是使第一句的内容更清楚具体，保证读者能够准确理解。

3. 段落层次

在段落层次上，上段中出现的信息在下段中可能要进行重述或部分重述，作者这样做的目的是帮助读者紧跟文章的行文思路。例如：

In a single classroom, desk-top computers will enable students to work at their own speeds and on different subjects at the same time. New research indicates young brains grow in spurts- not as a steady, continuous pace, as previously thought. As a result, school curricula will be tailored to match stages of brain development.

Skills such as mathematical reasoning will be emphasized in the age groups 2-4, 6-8, 10-12 and 14-16; when the brains expanding rapidly, rather than at plateau phases when the brain handle these tasks as well.

译文：在一间教室里安装台式电脑，就能保证学生们按自己的速度，同时学习不同科目的课程。新的研究结果表明，孩子们的大脑会突然快速发育，而不是像人们所想象的以稳定持续的速度发育。所以学校的课程安排要与学生大脑发育的阶段性相适应。

诸如数学推理一类的技能将在大脑发育很快的时期予以重视，即2~4岁、6~8岁、10~12岁、14~16岁这几个年龄段，而不是在智力发展停滞阶段才强调，因为这个阶段大脑处理此任务的能力已不如上述时期。

例子中第二段的 the brain is expanding rapidly 就是重述第一段中 young brains grow in spurts 的意思，并使第一段中这个意思表达得更加清楚明确。

（二）冗余信息在不同语言运用中的表现

冗余信息在不同的语言运用中表现也不同。在英语阅读中，冗余信息是针对作者通过篇章向读者传达的信息而言的，不是作者有意传达的信息都可认为是冗余信息。当然，这里所说的冗余信息不是绝对的，不是说这些信息是完全多余的，篇章中的大部分冗余信息能使篇章更连贯、流畅，更符合英语文体的需要。

1. 冗余信息与文体

有程式的公文文体往往不可避免地有一些长期保留下来的"繁文缛节"，负载冗余信息的行文较多；诗歌则要求精练，冗言较少。

2. 冗余信息与风格

正式或庄重场合的文章，在文字形式上要求比较严格，负载冗余信息的行文一般多于非正式场合的文章。

3. 冗余信息与对象

因为对象不同，对文章谈及的内容，有知之甚多、知之不多、知之甚少甚至一无所知几种情况。例如，在地铁里，一位对武汉情况一无所知的乘客听到"广埠屯"时会不知所云，但久住武汉的人，能马上反应出来这个词的含义；再如写日记，日记是写给自己看的，所以可以省略很多的冗余信息。

另外，冗余信息也因交际场合、句式安排、语势节奏等方面的不同而不同，要依据不同语言合理利用。

（三）分辨和利用冗余信息，提高阅读理解能力

冗余度较高的文体比较简单易懂。但是冗余度过高则使文本枯燥无味，缺乏吸引力，冗余度太低就会使文本晦涩难懂，使读者丧失兴趣。信息冗余可有助于解决信息过载与读者信道容量相对狭窄的矛盾。冗余又是确保信息正确传输的一个有效手段，在整个信息传输过程中，抑制"噪音"等各种干扰因素，并使信息准确无误地传输的一个最有效的办法就是增加信息冗余的编码。

在很多情况下，在汉语所处的文化传统中缺乏英语所隐含的地理、历史、政治、经济、习俗、价值观等文化因素，我们很难在汉语中找到英语的等值词语。因此，要想使汉语文本和英语文本达到意义上的绝对对等是不可能的，只能做到在某种程度上的相对对等，即美国语言学家尤金·奈达教授提出的动态对等（dynamic equivalence）。其主要原因是一般外语读者的信道接受力（channel capacity）会远远小于原语读者的信道接受力。

那么，为什么会出现这种现象？每个语言信息的传递都具有两个平面——长度和难度。信息必须通过读者的接收通道，才能为读者所接受。在交际活动中，任何结构适当的原文信息都会与原文读者的信道接受力相符合。但是，英语和汉语在语言本身和文化背景上存在巨大的差异，两种语符在转换过程中往往会破坏原语信道之间固有的平衡，即原语内容和形式与原语读者接受能力之间的吻合，成为阻碍汉语文本读者做出相同反应的障碍。克服这种障碍的办法往往就是在阅读时增加一些必要的成分，即信息冗余成分，这种信息冗余因素可以使可能出现的语义过载和形式过载问题得到缓解。

对于冗余信息太少的文本，我们为了更好地理解原语文本往往降低原语文本的信息负载难度。只有我们的信息负载与其信道相吻合时，信息的传输才能够通畅，我们也才能比较轻松地理解其文本的意义。而在保持信息内容不变的情况下，降低信息负载难度就意味着要加大信息的长度，也就是要在阅读理解与欣赏过程中适当增加一些使原语意义更加浅显化、更加表面化和更加明晰化的词语，即适当增加信息冗余度来打通其信道，以便我们更容易理解。

这里必须强调的一点就是：在拉长信息表达形式时，我们不能任意增加信息内容，而只可把原语文本中那些"不言而喻"的内隐成分加以处理。也就是说，我们增加文本的信息冗余度，并不意味着可以随意增加原语文本没有的信息，只是将信息从隐含的层面提升到表面。

另外，对于冗余信息过多的文本，有效分辨和利用阅读材料中的冗余信息有助于我们分清主要信息、次要信息和冗余信息，这对于正确理解阅读材料并提高阅读速度来讲非常关键。

分辨冗余信息要求我们在阅读过程中找出关键词，寻读关键词相关内容，以求抓住文章梗概，概括文章大意。可以有选择地进行跳跃式阅读，而不是逐词阅读，跳过一些无用的信息，抓住有用信息，从而加快速度，提高阅读效率。为了实现这个目标，我们可以采用以下四种方法：通读文章的首段和尾段，细读其他段落的主题句、首句和尾句，浏览与主题句相关的信息词，跳过其他次要内容，特别是冗余信息。

阅读理解，特别是快速阅读理解，要求我们从较长的文字资料中查找特定的细节，也就是进行扫视，以最快的速度从文章中获得有用的信息。

我们可以利用冗余现象有选择地捕捉最重要的语言线索。比如，一篇阅读理解中有这样一段话：Then there's the ostrich approach. "Some men are scared of what might be there and would rather not know," says Dr.Ross Cartmill.

其中一道题目是：

What does Dr. Ross Cartmill mean by "the ostrich approach"?

A. A casual attitude towards one's health conditions.

B. A new therapy for certain psychological problems.

C. Refusal to get medical treatment for fear of the pain involved.

D. Unwillingness to find out about one's disease because of fear.

这道题目中"the ostrich approach"的意思完全可以由其下句"Some men are scared of what might be there and would rather not know"推断出，即一些人害怕自己可能会有什么问题，所以他们宁愿不知道。利用这一冗余信息我们可以确定选项 D 就是正确答案。

除此之外，预测对于阅读理解也很重要。在进行阅读练习时，利用上下文、构词法等冗余信息预测文意，带着问题阅读文章，有利于提高阅读速度，增强对于文章的理解。而且，猜测生词词义是扩大词汇量的有效方法。

六、判断与推理

（一）寻找暗示

在学会阅读中心思想及寻找具体细节后，需要提高深一层次的能力。有时作者不直截了当地把想说的东西告诉读者，或是由于写作风格的需要，或是作者认为读者能间接理解自己的意思，所以没有直接、明确地陈述，但希望读者领悟，在阅读中称为推论。

在阅读时，有时要明白作者隐藏在表面现象下的意思，即隐含意思。读者要透过字里行间去理解作者的意思，也就是通常说的言外之意，这在英语中称为

read between the lines 或 understand the implied meaning。

作者通过词汇来暗示他所想表达的言外之意，因此在阅读时，应该仔细推敲作者的用词。另外，读者应该寻找一些事实根据，此时，读者就像是个侦探，根据时间、地点、态度、气氛、理由、结果、情感、方法等线索做出综合分析，合理推理，就像清晨醒来，推窗看一下行人身上穿什么衣服，我们就能判断外面的温度。

推论有时很简单明了，如"Dogs were barking all night"可以暗示"many sleepless neighbors"，也可能是"many angry neighbors"，导致合乎逻辑的"phone calls, letters to the editors and perhaps police station"，即打电话、写信投诉，甚至叫警方干预。

推论有时不那么明了，比如政治家演说中的暗示、法律条文的细微差别等，只有利用上下文线索，仔细研究才能明白。要做一个挑剔的读者，要提高推理能力。第一，必须弄懂字面意思；第二，必须透过字面意思去思考。读者要学会寻找暗示线索，并与已知事实联系起来。注意推理时应该以作者所描述的事实为依据，不能凭空想象。只有仔细阅读，全面思考问题，才能从表面的意思中，合乎逻辑地理解出深层次的意思。

作者在描述事实时往往带有自己的观点，有时赞成，有时反对，有时客观，有时主观。读者在阅读时应该把握住这个重点，可以通过看作者的用词来判断他的观点，如果他用的褒义词多，他一定持支持、赞成的观点，反之，一定持批评、不赞成的观点。

经常提问有关作者观点的词汇有：

positive（积极的；肯定的）、negative（消极的；否定的）、neutral（中立的）、critical（批判的）、objective（客观的）、subjective（主观的）、pessimistic（悲观的）、optimistic（乐观的）、doubtful（怀疑的）、indifferent（冷漠的；不关心的）、compromising（妥协的）、hostile（敌对的）等。

（二）难点分析

Passage 1

In the living room, the grandmother sat in her usual chair. She looked down at her lap while one hand absently stroked the other. The mother pressed the drip-dry men's shits, one after the other, and hung them on hangers. Every few minutes she glanced at the wall clock, with a worried twitch of her eyebrows. Davey, the ten-year-old, ran into the room and tuned on the television. But the mother pushed past him, snapped it off, and gritted between her teeth, "You can't have that tube on tonight!" He opened his mouth in surprise, then turned and ran out, slamming the door. Once again, the iron thumped, the shirt hangers clanked. To the two women, the hands of the clock seemed to be stopped.

1. What is the main idea of this paragraph?

2. What are some of the stated details?

3. What are some of the unstated facts?

Example: The wearer of the shirts——the father? ——is not home.

4. What inferences can you make about this situation?

5. What inferences are unsupported?

这段短文的中心思想与作者描述的气氛密切相关。母亲在默默地熨烫衣服，祖母心神不定，不时看着钟，似乎在等候什么人。文中还提到一个 10 岁的孩子，他不能看他平时喜欢看的电视节目，母亲甚至还对小男孩儿大发脾气，可小男孩儿蒙在鼓里，一无所知。

进一步的思考，我们会发问：他们在等谁？衬衫的主人？男孩儿的父亲？他这么晚还没回家，发生了什么事？看来是令人担心的事，因为作者描述的整个气氛令人压抑，以上这些是合乎逻辑的推论。

当然我们不能作无根据的推论，如父亲失业了，去酗酒了，回家后大发雷霆，乱打妻子；更不能乱发挥想象力，接着两位妇女及男孩儿被抓、扣作人质等，因为这样的推理没有事实根据。

以上问题的参考答案：

1. A nervous waiting by two women.

2. Three people are mentioned: a mother who is ironing silently, a grandmother who is sitting silently, and a ten-year-old who is not allowed to watch his usual TV

program. The mother watched the clock anxiously, and so on.

3. The two women share the same feeling of anxiety. The mother seems irritated by the ten-year old's behavior. He must usually watch TV, since he seems surprised at being scolded.

4. Someone—the father? —is late coming home. Something is about to happen, which the women know about and expect but the ten-year-old doesn't. It is not a pleasant thing—all the details express tension in the air.

5. Father has lost his job and is coming home in a drunken rage to beat his family. Or the child is being held hostage by a murderer.

Passage 2

Nursing at Beth Israel hospital produces the best patient care possible. If we are to solve the nursing shortage , hospital administration and doctors everywhere would do well to follow Beth Israel's example.

At Beth Israel each patient is assigned to a primary nurse who visits at length with the patient and constructs a full-scale health account that covers everything from his medical history to his emotional state. Then she writes a care plan centered on the patient's illness but which also includes everything else that is necessary.

The primary nurse stays with the patient through his hospitalization, keeping track with his progress and seeking further advice from his doctor. If a patient at Beth Israel is not responding to treatment, it is not uncommon for his nurse to propose another approach to his doctor. What the doctor at Beth Israel has in the primary nurse is a true colleague.

Nursing at Beth Israel also involves a decentralized nursing administration; every floor, every unit is a self-contained organization. There are nurse-managers instead of head nurses; in addition to their medical duties they do all their own hiring and dismissing, employee advising, and they make salary recommendations. Each unit's nurses decide among themselves who will work what shifts and when.

Beth Israel's nurse -in-chief ranks as an equal with other vice presidents of the hospital. She also is a member of the Medical Executive Committee, which in most hospitals includes only doctors.

1. Which of the following best characterizes the main feature of the nursing system at Beth Israel Hospital?

A. The doctor gets more active professional support from the primary nurse.

B. Each patient is taken care of by a primary nurse day and night.

C. The primary nurse writes care plans for every patient.

D. The primary nurse keeps records of the patient's health conditions every day.

2. It can be inferred from the passage that ____.

A. compared with other hospitals nurses at Beth Israel Hospital are more patient

B. in most hospitals patient care is inadequate from the professional point of view

C. in most hospitals nurses get low salaries

D. compared with other hospitals nurses have to work longer hours at Beth Israel Hospital

3. A primary nurse can propose a different approach of treatment when ____.

A. the present one is refused by the patient

B. the patient complains about the present one

C. the present one proves to be ineffective

D. the patient is found unwilling to cooperate

4. The main difference between a nurse manager and a head nurse is that the former ____.

A. is a member of the Medical Executive Committee of the hospital

B. has to arrange the work shifts of the unit's nurses

C. can make decisions concerning the medical treatment of a patient

D. has full responsibility in the administration of the unit's nurses

5. The author's attitude towards the nursing system at Beth Israel Hospital is ____.

A. negative

B. critical

C. neutral

D. positive

这篇文章介绍了一家为病人提供优质服务的医院。在第一段提出话题之后，后面几段分别叙述了这家医院的特色，全文表达了作者对这家医院的赞赏。文章传递的信息是：如要解决护理工作不足的问题，大家应向这家医院学习。

1. A 项是正确答案。这是一道概括题，与本文的中心思想有关，依据在第三段最后一句。"characterizes the main feature"是"表示……的特征"的意思。文中提到医生与责任护士的关系是这家医院的特色。其他选项是护士的常规工作，没有什么与众不同的地方。

2. B 项是正确答案。这是一道推论题，依据在第一段最后一句。文中提到如要解决护理工作不足的问题，就应向这家医院学习，言下之意是目前护理工作确实做得不到位，否则也没有必要提出这个话题。根据文本，无从得出这家医院的护士"更耐心""工作时间较长"，其他医院护士"工资较低"的结论。

3. C 项是正确答案。依据在第三段第二句。题干中的 the present one proves to be ineffective 对应文中的"If a patient is not responding to treatment..."，即"当前的治疗方案无效"的意思。注意这里有个双重否定的结构：not uncommon，表示肯定的意思，即护士通常会这么做。其他选项"病人拒绝""病人投诉""病人不愿合作"都不对。

4. D 项是正确答案。依据在第四段，本段的主题句介绍了这家医院有分散的护理管理制度，接着以例子说明护士主管与护士长的区别，前者更多地参与管理。本文的主题是介绍一家特色医院，应该领悟作者提到的与众不同的地方。粗心的人会把第五段中的 nurse-in-chief（首席护士）当成 nurse-manager，故误选 C 项。

5. D 项是正确答案。这是一道概括作者态度的题目。第一段第二句号召大家向这家医院学习，当然是肯定这家医院的做法，后面几段把这家医院与众不同的特色描写出来，表达了作者赞赏的态度。

第二节 阅读教学与评价

一、过程性评价

（一）过程性评价的目的与内容

1. 过程性评价的目的

过程性评价的目的是激发学生的学习动力，通过评价，使学生在阅读活动的条件和氛围内不断体验进步与成功，认识自我，建立自信。对自己的学习方法和进步情况进行不断反思，及时而有效地调控自己的学习过程，并形成有效的学习策略，促进学生综合运用语言能力的全面发展，使学生具有良好的阅读能力。培养学生从学会学习到学会评价，并能正确对待自己和他人的评价结果，学会尊重他人。通过评价，形成积极的情感体验，并对教学形成积极的反馈作用，以调整教学计划和教学方法，改进教学策略。

2. 过程性评价的内容

阅读教学中的过程性评价主要是对日常教学进行的评价，包括学生的自主学习能力（如收集资料，分析、利用资料等）、小组协作过程中的交流与合作能力、学习策略和性格品质上的进步等。总之，要由教师和学生相互配合，共同协作完成。

（二）过程性评价的具体操作步骤

阅读训练旨在提高学生对英语阅读的兴趣，通过阅读学习，实现从"要我学"到"我要学"的转变。因此，不应该以传统的测试形式对学生进行评价，应设计出能客观、确切地反映出每个学生学习效果的评价方法。

1. 在学生实施阅读和评价过程中教师要监控和指导

教师在充分给予学生自主选择权的同时，要注意统一的管理和监控，不能放任自流。让学生自己选择阅读内容和方法、自己安排时间，充分发挥学生的自主性和个性化。同时，教师也要给予正确的指导、规定统一的时间周期、确定最小阅读量等。

第一，帮助学生制订切实可行的个人阅读计划，并将该计划存放在学生学习档案袋中，以备随时调整。

第二，指导学生的阅读方法。学生对阅读技巧知之甚少，教师要时时注意教授方法。比如，在培养学生的猜词能力时，教师可帮助学生分析推断词义的过程，其具体方法有：利用构词法来辨认同义词、反义词；利用关联词在文中的作用进行逻辑推断，把握其在语篇层次上所起的连接、指代、反证等作用，从而提高语篇分析能力。在进行阅读速度技能训练时，教师可提供速度技能训练，如略读和跳读等，通过扫描，迅速掌握篇章的主旨大意。另外，还可以通过训练学生阅读文章标题或第一段，形成对全篇内容的预测。在进行跳读时，学生对于希望获得的信息要有一个明确的认识，要带着问题去寻找答案，捕捉到所需的信息内容。

第三，提前布置阅读主题，让学生们查找报纸杂志或网络上有关的资料进行阅读，开展小组讨论，然后把自己的观点组织成文，在师生、学生间进行交流、讨论。教师也可通过读前活动将学生引入特定的情景中，找出阅读定位，通过标题或关键词启发学生已有的相关背景知识，也可以在读完一段后布置预测作品的其余内容。

第四，教师监控每单元进行的小组评价，时间为一节课。学生们可成立若干阅读小组，以4~5人为一个小组，参考教师布置的阅读主题，由组员选定阅读文章，读后在组内交流读书笔记并做好小组评价，填写评价表格。每组选一个小组长，每次评价时，小组的组长与被评价的对象相同，这样有利于组长和组员了解各成员的成长轨迹、发展状况和各自的进步与退步，所有的成员都应是评价者与被评价者。周小组评价表如表2-2-1所示。

表2-2-1 阅读教学中的过程性评价表（一）：周小组评价表

评价项目	评价内容	评价等级			
	被评价者姓名　第　周　星期　日期：年　月　日					
		一般	出色	优秀	良好	进步
完成阅读任务	具有较强的理解力，掌握其中心大意，抓住主要事实和有关细节					

续表

被评价者姓名　　第　周　星期　日期：年　月　日						
评价项目	评价内容	评价等级				
^	^	一般	出色	优秀	良好	进步
读书笔记/感受	学会搜集整理与阅读内容有关的词汇和背诵经典名句，学会写读后感					
阅读计划与监控	根据个人实际情况制订有效的阅读计划。明确预期达到的目标					
课外背景知识阅读	学会选择具有阅读价值的报刊、小说等课外读物进行阅读，课外阅读量每周约1000字，培养良好的阅读习惯					
阅读方法使用情况	反思自己阅读过程中的得失，不断优化个人学习策略，全面评价自己的学习					
参与小组活动	积极参与课外阅读活动，主动在活动中与人友好合作，乐于与人分享自己的劳动成果					
平时测验	在百分制计分中可分0～59分，60～64分，65～74分，75～84分，85～100分五个等级（150分计分以此类推）					
对待评价的态度	进行自我评价和评价他人时是否认真、客观、公正					
综合评价						
组长签名	教师签名	被评价者签名				

注：这种评价表只是过程性评价的形式之一，其他如平时的阅读技巧、参与竞赛的获奖情况等也应作为评价的内容

2.学生对自己的阅读进行自我监控和自我评估

自我监控和自我评估是学生将学习成果与自己的预设目标相对照的过程，是学生对阅读过程的反思和改进。

第一，学生在阅读过程中要学会记学习日记，记录当时的感受以及阅读后的反思等，并如实填写阅读自评表格。

第二，建立学习档案。学习档案可以帮助学生看到自己学习过程中的成果和进步，可以增强学生对学习的责任感。可将阅读计划、阅读笔记、阅读情况记录、反思等存放进去。

第三，根据实际，调整阅读计划。有时由于种种原因，学生预定的阅读计划未能实施，要根据实际情况调整阅读计划。阅读自评表如表 2-2-2 所示。

表 2-2-2　阅读教学中的过程性评价表（二）：月阅读自评表

月	阅读内容	取得的成绩	需要改进的方面
第一周			
第二周			
第三周			
第四周			
家长评价及建议			

注：①自我陈述的内容主要是对自己一段时间以来的表现进行详细描述，评价要真实、客观，并要对自己的阅读学习进行深入反思；②自评等级分为 A，B，C，D，E 五等；③要求用英语书写

二、形成性评价

在英语学习过程中，阅读作为重要的一环，对学生提高英语学习水平具有举足轻重的作用，以下就是阅读教学实施的基本过程：

（一）阅读前的活动

阅读前的活动可被视为新课的"导入"。教师运用启发手段，将问答、讨论等作为本课的话题导入内容，让学生了解话题的内容梗概。阅读课也应使用提问策略调动学生的学习积极性，培养他们的主体意识和参与意识。问答和讨论环节旨在激活学生永久记忆中相关的知识网络，使他们产生阅读的愿望和做好阅读的心理准备。

在学生首次阅读之前，教师提出指导性问题，其目的是给学生的首次阅读确定目标，实现对其阅读过程的监控。指导性问题同样可以指导学生了解课文的话题梗概，让其构建初步的、模糊的全文语义图像，帮助学生建立"自上而下"的信息加工机制。由于学生刚开始熟悉课文，并未运用课文中语言的能力，故教师设置指导性问题须涉及课文的主题或最重要的事实，学生回答问题的语言应力求简洁。

（二）阅读中的活动

本阶段的目的是使学生获取较详细的篇章信息，了解和熟悉课文中生疏的词汇、短语与结构等语言现象。在简短的首次阅读、检测和讨论其答案之后，学生已了解全文梗概。教师可使用快捷问题和适度的讲解、讨论来梳理全文信息和语言。在此过程中，教师应始终注意全文的语义中心，部分和整体的联系，尽可能使用一些直观手段，如用黑板或投影归纳全文内容的图解、表格等，帮助学生建构较详细的语义图像，以帮助学生基本理解课文内容。教师也可设置细节性问题或让学生填表等，让学生带着任务进行二次阅读，然后组织学生讨论并讲解。

讨论和讲解只应涉及关键点和难点，而不应逐词逐句进行。讨论或解释新的语言现象，可充分利用课文的语义中心和该语言现象的语境。此外，可适当举例或对比，但不可离开课文或中断学生的理解而进行无意义的扩展练习。

第二阶段的评价测试结果，可以是一份，也可是多份。根据阅读内容，教师可灵活掌握，目的是对学生给予全面、恰当的评价。

（三）阅读后的活动

此阶段侧重于学生对课文中语言形式的掌握和运用，对文章结构的分析以及文章的第二层次即意图层次的理解。首先，教师可组织学生做一些语言形式的基本练习，如本课需重点掌握的词汇、短语与结构等。练习的选择和设置应注意语言形式与意义的联系。然后，教师可根据本阶段的目的选择活动形式，旨在让学生进一步熟悉课文内容，巩固所学的语言形式，认识语篇的结构层次和意图层次，并学会创造性地运用本课所掌握的语言形式。

三、多维评价体系

以形成性评价为主的多维评价体系在阅读教学中的实施分为诊断性评价、形成性评价以及终结性评价的实施。以一学期为例，诊断性评价可以在学期初进行，终结性评价可以在学期末进行，在这期间的整个教学过程中实施形成性评价。

(一)诊断性评价实施

在一个学期开始的第一周,对学生的阅读能力、词汇水平等认知能力和学习动机、学习态度等情感因素进行诊断性的评价。运用标准化测试考查学生的阅读水平,运用调查问卷了解学生的情感因素。为了保证其信度和效度,标准化水平测试的试题可以选取大学英语四级考试中的阅读部分。

(二)形成性评价的实施

形成性评价是多维评价体系中的重要环节,其评价方式也多种多样,可以采用自我评价/学生互评、建立学生学习档案、教师日常记录、访谈等多种形式的评价方式,在该学期的教学中实施。

1. 自我评价/学生互评

自我评价的意义在于学生可以通过自我评价发现学习中的优点和不足,并以此为依据改进学习目标,调整学习策略;教师也可以依照学生在自我评价中反映出的问题合理安排教学重点,完善教学计划,有的放矢地给每个学生提供有效的帮助。学生互评可以让学生意识到"同伴文化"的力量以及友好气氛在学习过程中的重要性。自我评价的标准主要设定为对阅读中认知策略使用的评估,如计划、选择注意、监控、评价等方面。由于学生对阅读中的认知策略可能缺乏了解,自我评估的项目应当主要由教师来制定,评价分为优、良、中、差四个级别。教师可以根据评价类别、具体的评价项目和评价等级制成自我评价表,要求学生每周对自己的阅读进行一次自我评价,并且由学生本人如实地填写。具体的评价内容包括以下四点:

第一,计划:能够制定长期和短期的阅读目标、能够根据阅读目标找出符合自己水平的读物、能够制订阅读计划(如规定一定时期的阅读量等)、能够根据不同的文章考虑运用不同的阅读方法和策略。

第二,选择注意:先快速浏览一遍文章,待了解要点后再仔细阅读;阅读开始时根据文章的标题预测文章的内容;阅读时通过做记号来突出重点,并帮助自己回忆内容;阅读时注意并利用注释帮助自己理解文章内容;阅读时注意文章段落的主题句,并借此判断主旨或大意。

第三,监督:阅读过程中停下来思考、检查自己是否理解所读内容;阅读过程中自我提问，并通过阅读找到答案；阅读过程中根据所读内容修正先前的预测；阅读过程中及时检查所用的阅读方法是否恰当，及时调整不当的方法；阅读过程中根据阅读时间和阅读量调整阅读速度。

第四，评价：阅读后评价自己对文章的理解程度如何；阅读后评价自己对文章的看法，而非完全接受；阅读后总结所使用的阅读方法或策略是否有助于文章的理解；阅读后评价所读的文章是否满足自己的阅读目标或要求；阅读后评价自己有哪些收获；阅读后找出自己的弱点，并考虑今后的改进措施。

学生互评主要针对学生在阅读课堂上的表现、参加小组活动情况等项目进行考察。评价项目由学生和教师共同制定，评价标准与自我评价相同，分为优、良、中、差四项。学生互评表的评价项目可以包括：根据需要进行预习（了解背景知识，预习词汇）；主动回答教师提出的问题；在课堂上认真做好笔记，善于把握要点；遇到不清楚的环节能主动向教师提问；经常与教师和同学交流阅读策略和方法；积极主动参加小组讨论；按时认真完成课堂上的作业；阅读课的出勤情况等。学生互评后还要针对学生的优点、缺点进行点评，并对出现的问题提出改进建议。

2. 建立学生学习档案

学生学习档案用来收集学生一个阶段或一个学期的学习成就。这些资料能显示学生的学习态度、努力程度、学生的发展与进步。学生学习档案的内容主要包括：课前预习时准备的材料。内容可以是对将要学到的课文的文化、历史等背景知识的介绍，对生词的预习，对文章结构和理解方面存在的问题。形式可以是手写的或打印的书面资料，可以是 MP3 播放器、也可以是光盘、移动存储设备上的视频资料。根据准备材料的数量和内容的质量加以评估。课外阅读材料，写读书报告或阅读笔记。阅读材料包括课外阅读的英文报纸、杂志、文学读物等，选择其中的部分英文读物或英文文章写读书报告或阅读笔记。根据阅读的文字量、阅读理解情况及阅读笔记或读书报告的写作情况给予综合评价。学生对于阅读策略的总结。学生对于阅读不同类型文章时使用的方法和技巧进行归纳和总结。教师对学生阅读技巧的掌握和使用做出评价。

3. 教师日常记录

教师通过观察学生在日常学习中的表现对学生进行记录，内容包括：通过提问的方式检验学生课前预习的情况，学生在课堂上发言、参与课堂活动的情况，学生对篇章理解的情况，学生阅读策略的使用情况，学生课后完成作业情况，还有对学生取得的进步的纪实性描述。

4. 访谈

教师通过访谈的形式，对学生的个人进步和需求做出正确和积极的评估。访谈中提出的问题可以是：你在阅读中会采取哪些阅读策略？你在阅读后会不会对整个阅读过程进行总结？你认为阅读中的难点是什么？你在进行课外阅读的时候喜欢选择哪类读物？每周花在阅读上的时间大概有多少？学生的回答可以帮助教师及时了解学生存在的问题和学生取得的进步，以便教师为总结教学中出现的问题及制订下一步的教学计划提供指导和参照。

（三）终结性评价的实施

在该学期的教学过程结束后，再次运用标准化水平测试，对整个阶段学生的学习效果进行评价。试题仍然是从大学英语四级考试中选取的阅读理解题，但是选取的阅读内容应与上次不同，以免影响评价效果。

以形成性评价为主，诊断性评价、形成性评价与终结性评价相结合的多维评价体系是符合大学英语改革理念的全面的、综合性的评价方式。它有利于确立学生在整个教学过程中的主体地位，有利于学生课内外认知能力、学习策略以及态度、动机、情感等方面的培养。以形成性评价为主的多维评价体系为教师们提供了一个更全面地反映学生学习能力和表现的评价方式，但是由于形成性评价的内容、标准、评分方式在操作中很难统一，这种教学评价的实施也给教师们带来了新的挑战。

第三节 阅读训练

一、Reading 1

Directions: There are 2 passages in this section. Each passage is followed by some questions or unfinished statements. For each of them, there are four choices marked (A), (B), (C) and (D). You should decide which is the best answer.

Passage One

Questions 1 to 5 are based on the following passage.

The process of perceiving other people is rarely translated into cold, objective terms. "She was 5 feet 8 inches tall, had fair hair, and wore a colored skirt." More often, we try to get inside the other person to pinpoint his or her attitudes, emotions, motivations, abilities, ideas and characters. Furthermore, we sometimes behave as if we ca accomplish this difficult job very quickly—perhaps with a two-second glance.

We try to obtain information about others in many ways. Berger suggests several methods for reducing uncertainties about others: watching, without being noticed, a person interacting with others, particularly with others who are known to you, so you can compare the observed person's behavior with the known other's behavior; observing a person in a situation where social behavior is relatively unrestrained or where a wide variety of behavioral responses are called for; deliberately structuring the physical or social environment so as to observe the person's responses to specific stimuli; asking people who have had or have frequent contact with the person about him or her; and using various strategies in face-to-face interaction to uncover information about another person—questions, self-disclosures, and so on. Getting to know someone is a never-ending task, largely because people are constantly changing and the methods we use to obtain information are often imprecise. You may have known someone for ten years and still know very little about him. If we accept the idea that we won't ever fully know another person, it enables us to deal more easily with those things that get in the way of accurate knowledge such as secrets and deceptions. It will also keep us from being too surprised by seemingly inconsistent behavior. Ironically, those things that keep us from knowing another person too well (e.g. secrets and deceptions) may be just as important to the development of a satisfying relationship as the things that enable us to obtain accurate knowledge about a person (e.g. disclosures and truthful statements).

1. The word "pinpoint" (Para. 1) basically means ____.

A. appreciate

B. obtain

C. interpret

D. identify

2. What do we learn from the first paragraph?

A. People are better described in cold, objective terms.

B. The difficulty of getting to know a person is usually underestimated.

C. One should not judge people by their appearances.

D. One is usually subjective when assessing other people's personality.

3. It can be inferred from Berger's suggestions that ____.

A. people do not reveal their true self on every occasions

B. in most cases we should avoid contacting the observed person directly

C. the best way to know a person is by making comparisons

D. face-to-face interaction is the best strategy to uncover information about a person

4. In developing personal relationships, secrets and deceptions, in the author's opinion, are ____.

A. personal matters that should be seriously dealt with

B. barriers that should be done away with

C. as significant as disclosures and truthful statements

D. things people should guard against

5. The author's purpose in writing the passage is ____.

A. to give advice on appropriate conduct for social occasions

B. to provide ways of how to obtain information about people

C. to call the reader's attention to the negative side of people's characters

D. to discuss the various aspects of getting to know people

［注释］

pinpoint：明确指出；确定；准确描述

unrestrained：无限制的；放纵的；自然的

self-disclosure：自我表露

imprecise：不精确的；不严密的；不确切的

deception：欺骗；欺诈；骗术

ironically：讽刺地；说反话地

Passage Two

Questions 6 to 10 are based on the following passage.

A wise man once said that the only thing necessary for the triumph of evil is for good men to do nothing. So, as a police officer, I have some urgent things to say to good people.

Days after days my men and I struggle to hold back a tidal wave of crime. Something has gone terribly wrong with our once-proud American way of life. It has happened in the area of values. A key ingredient is disappearing, and I think I know what it is: accountability.

Accountability isn't hard to define. It means that every person is responsible for his or her actions and liable for their consequences.

Of the many values that hold civilization together—honesty, kindness, and so on—accountability may be the most important of all. Without it, there can be no respect, no trust, no law—and, ultimately, no society.

My job as a police officer is to impose accountability on people who refuse, or have never learned, to impose it on themselves. But as every policeman knows, external controls on people's behavior are far less effective than internal restrains such as guilt, shame and embarrassment.

Fortunately there are still : communities—smaller towns, usually—where schools maintain discipline and where parents hold up standards that proclaim: "In this family certain things are not tolerated—they simply are not done!"

Yet more and more, especially in our larger cities and suburbs, these inner restraints are loosening. Your typical robber has none. He considers your property his property; he takes what he wants, including your life if you enrage him.

The main cause of this break-down is a radical shift in attitudes. Thirty years ago, if a crime was committed, society was considered the victim. Now, in a shocking reversal, it's the criminal who is considered victimized: by his underprivileged upbringing, by the school that didn't teach him to read, by the church that failed to reach him with moral guidance, by the parents who didn't provide a stable home.

I don't believe it. Many others in equally disadvantaged circumstances choose not to engage in criminal activities. If we free the criminal, even partly, from accountability, we become a society of endless excuses where no one accepts responsibility for anything.

We in American desperately need more people who believe that the person who commits a crime is the one responsible for it.

1. What the wise man said suggests that _____.

A. it is necessary for good people to do nothing in face of danger

B. it is important for good people to keep away from evil

C. it is natural that good people will defeat bad people

D. it is certain that something bad will prevail if good men do nothing in face of it

2. According to the author, if a person is found guilty of a crime, _____.

A. families and schools are to be blamed for it

B. society is responsible for it

C. the living conditions should be improved

D. the criminal himself should bear the blame

3. Compared with those in small towns, people in large cities have ____.

A. less self-discipline

B. worse living conditions

C. better sense of responsibility

D. more mutual respect

4. The author is sorry to have noticed that ____.

A. people in small towns still stick to discipline

B. people in large cities tend to free the criminal from accountability

C. many people in disadvantaged circumstance are not engaged in criminal activities

D. people lack sympathy for people in disadvantaged circumstances

5. What's the main idea of the passage?

A. More people should accept the value of accountability.

B. Good men should do more in face of evil.

C. Stricter discipline should be maintained in schools and families.

D. Every policeman should impose more accountability on people who refuse.

[注释]

ingredient：要素；组成部分；原料

proclaim：声明；宣告；公布；表明；赞扬

reversal：逆转；撤销

二、Reading 2

Long before the first visitor bought a flowered shirt, Hawaiians stood in awe of a natural resource more powerful than tourism, ——the virtually unlimited energy force buried deep within the conical volcanic mountains of the island of Hawaii.

Turning fantasy into reality , geothermal experts from the Federal Department of

Energy, the Hawaiian Electric Light Company and the state of Hawaii are building a $6.8 million power plant to capture water boiling at 570 degrees Fahrenheit from the depths of the active Kilauea Volcano and use it to generate inexpensive electricity.

It will work like this: Deep wells will be drilled to reach underground water heated by volcanic pressure. Once the water is tapped and channeled into pipelines, the pressure will be released, changing the water to steam. By the time it reaches ground level, the vapor will be 99 percent steam and 400 degrees Fahrenheit.

The plan calls for installing small portable power plants at the drilling sites while the energy potential of the reservoir is established and, by 1980, the construction of a permanent power plant which will use a turbine to convert the steam into electricity.

But volcanoes are still tricky to tame, so scientists are building failsafe mechanisms. The plant will be engineered to withstand volcanic-triggered earthquakes measuring up to 9 points on the Richter Scale. And to prevent Lava（熔岩）burial, the power plant will be barricaded by walls to deflect lava flows around it.

1. How long has Hawaii's natural energy resource been known?

A. Up to very recently.

B. By the end of 1980.

C. Long before outsiders visited the islands.

D. After the volcano erupted.

2. Which of the following is not mentioned about the joint effort of exploiting the natural resource?

A. Kilauea Volcano Plant.

B. Federal Department of Energy.

C. Hawaiian Electric Light Company.

D. State of Hawaii.

3. What is the purpose of the power plant?

A. To make more flower shirts to develop tourism industry.

B. To obtain boiling water to produce cheap electricity.

C. To build strong walls to prevent lava burial.

D. To get underground drinking water for the local villagers.

4. When a turbine is used in the power plant, ____.

A. it drills water from the underground

B. it captures pressure in a volcano

C. it changes water into steam

D. it changes steam into electricity

5. What is the function of paragraph 5 in this passage?

A. States the main idea of the passage.

B. Gives a general description of the project.

C. Describes unique features of the plan.

D. Describes potential problems and how to solve them.

三、Reading 3

This spectacular sight awaits Falmouth in Cornwall at 11:11 am, Wednesday, August 11, 1999, as the eclipse, which starts at 9:57 am, reaches totality. Viewers will have 2 minutes 6 seconds to observe it. The total eclipse will also take in the Scilly Isles, the mainland south of a line from St Just to Teignmouth and Aldernery.

The moon's orbit takes it directly between the earth and the sun casting a shadow of total darkness about 75 miles across. The Sun is blocked exactly by the Moon, because although it is 400 times large than the Moon, it is also 400 times further from Earth.

Don't look at the sun directly without special glasses. The sun's rays can cause permanent blindness. Project it on to a card with a pinhole camera, or watch it on television or the Internet. If you use special glasses, make sure they are not damaged.

On Wednesday most of Britain will be overcast, including 85 % of Cornwall and 75% of Devon. Dropping temperatures may clear the cloud. Best views of the partial eclipse will be in the southeast.

BBC broadcasts from Penzance Bay at 9.45. ITV and Sky start at 10. Pictures filmed from planes will ensure a good view. Websites: try www.eclipse.org.uk or www.eclipsecast.com. Pictures from space are on www.eumetsat.

You won't get another chance until June 2001, when you'll have to go to southern Africa. The next in Britain is not until 2090.

1. According to the passage, the best time for viewers at Cornwall to see the total eclipse is at ____.

A. 11:11 am

B. 9:45 am

C. 9:57 am

D. 10 am

2. How does eclipse happen?

A. The moon is blocked completely by the earth.

B. The earth is blocked completely by the moon.

C. The sun is blocked completely by the moon.

D. The sun is blocked completely by the earth.

3. Viewers are advised not to ____.

A. watch about eclipse on television broadcast at home

B. project the light of the sun through a pinhole on to a white card

C. look at the sun directly without a pair of special glasses

D. view live coverage by World Wide Web cameras on Internet

4. What is the weather like when eclipse happens in Cornwall?

A. Fine.

B. Bad.

C. Cold.

D. Rainy.

5. Why is this eclipse a spectacular event for British people?

A. Because the eclipse happens only once in a blue moon.

B. Because the one in Britain is better than that in other countries.

C. Because the heavenly magic show attracts hundreds of adventurous viewers to their countries.

D. Because they won't eyewitness another one in Britain until 91 years later.

四、Reading 4

The Mixed - ability Teaching

We find that bright children are rarely held back by mixed-ability teaching. On the contrary, both their knowledge and experience are enriched. We feel that there are many disadvantages in streaming pupils. It can have a bad effect on both the bright and the not-so-bright child. After all, it can be quite discouraging to be at the bottom of the top grade.

Besides, it's rather unreal to grade people just according to their intellectual ability. This is only one aspect of their total personality. We are concerned to develop the abilities of all our pupils to the full, not just their academic ability. We also value personal qualities and social skills, and we find that mixed - ability teaching contributes to all these aspects of learning.

In our classrooms, we work in various ways. The pupils often work in groups; this gives them the opportunity to learn to co-operate, to share, and to develop leadership skills. They also learn how to cope with personal problems as well as learning how to think, to make decisions, to analyze and evaluate, and to communicate effectively. The pupils learn from each other as well as from the teacher.

Sometimes the pupils work in pairs; sometimes they work on individual tasks and assignments, and they can do this at their own speed. They also have some formal class teaching when this is appropriate. We encourage our pupils to use the library, and we teach them the skills they need in order to do this efficiently. We expect our pupils to do their best, not their least, and we give every encouragement to attain this goal.

1. In the passage the author's attitude towards "mixed-ability teaching" is _____.

A. critical

B. questioning

C. approving

D. objective

2. The word "streaming" in Para. 1 probably means _____.

A. flowing freely

B. waving in the wind

C. teaching pupils to swim in the stream or in the swimming pool

D. placing the pupils in groups according to ability and intelligence

3. The author argues that a teacher's chief concern should be the development of the student's _____.

A. academic ability

B. total personality

C. learning ability and communicative skills

D. intellectual ability

4. Which of the following is NOT mentioned in the third paragraph?

A. Pupils learn to work together with others.

B. Pupils also learn to develop their reasoning abilities.

C. Pupils learn to be capable organizers.

D. Pupils also learn how to participate in teaching activities.

5. What is the main idea of Para. 4?

A. The way of teaching in mixed-ability class.

B. Children have freedom in study.

C. Pupils are encouraged to do their best.

D. The advantage of group work.

第三章　英语写作学习策略与指导

写作课是大学英语基础阶段结束后，英语提高阶段中的一门重要课程。随着我国加入世界贸易组织（WTO），社会及用人单位对大学毕业生的英语实用交际能力越来越看重。本章节主要介绍了句子写作、段落写作、篇章写作以及写作技巧。

第一节　句子写作

一、句子基本结构

句子是人们表达思想、进行交际的基本语言单位。好的英语句子用词准确、结构严谨、表达通顺、逻辑严密，能准确、有效、生动地传递信息和表达思想。一个完整的英语句子必须具备两个成分：主语和谓语。

谓语部分的核心是动词，英语动词使用和分类是根据动词的特性来决定的。一般情况下，动词可以分为以下几类：

第一，根据其后是否带有宾语，动词分为及物动词（Transitive Verb，缩写形式为 vt.）和不及物动词（Intransitive Verb，缩写形式为 vi.）。同一动词可具有及物动词和不及物动词两种特性。

第二，根据其在句中的功能，动词可分为四类：实义动词（Notional Verb）、系动词（Linking Verb）、助动词（Auxiliary Verb）和情态动词（Modal Verb）。

第三，根据是否受主语的人称和数的限制，动词可分为：限定动词（Finite Verb）和非限定动词（Non-finite Verb）。

谓语动词用法的复杂性决定了英语句子表述的多样性，但千变万化的句子归根结底都是由五个基本句型变化而来的。因此，只有把这五个基本句型掌握好，才能运用英语进行清楚、准确地表达。

通常，根据行文和表述的需要，可以把简单句合并成复杂的句式，并由此产生了并列句和复合句。

（一）四种英语句子（按用途分）

1. 陈述句（Declarative Sentence）

肯定句：My daughter is six this year.

否定句：Kate has not heard from her cousin since last year.

2. 疑问句（Interrogative Sentence）

一般疑问句：Do you like playing football?

特殊疑问句：What is your name?

选择疑问句：Is his son five or seven years old?

反义疑问句：It is a lovely day, isn't it?

3. 祈使句（Imperative Sentence）

肯定式：Please be quiet, boys!

否定式：Don't eat in class!

4. 感叹句（Exclamatory Sentence）

How 一式：How time flies!

What 一式：What a clever boy he is!

（二）三种英语句子（按结构分）

（1）简单句（Simple Sentence）

简单句由一个主语（或并列主语）（用 S 表示）和一个谓语（或并列谓语）组成。

例如：

① Middle school students often read English in the morning.
　　　　　　（S）　　　　　　（V）

② <u>Tom and Mike</u> <u>are</u> good friends.
　　（S）　　（V）

③ <u>The little boy</u> <u>likes</u> drawing and often <u>draws</u> pictures for the wall-newspaper at school.
　　（S）　　（V₁）　　　　　　　　（V₂）

（2）并列句（Compound Sentence）

并列句由两个或两个以上简单句组成，通常使用并列连词 and、but、or 等。例如：

<u>My father is a teacher</u> and <u>my mother is an office-employee.</u>
（Simple Sentence 1）　　　（Simple Sentence 2）

<u>The future is bright</u> and <u>the road is tortuous.</u>
（Simple Sentence 1）　（Simple Sentence 2）

（3）复合句（Complex Sentence）

复合句由一个主句（Principal Clause）和一个或一个以上的从句（Subordinate Clause）组成。

主句是全句的主体，通常可以独立存在。而从句则是一个句子成分，不能独立存在。从句虽然不能独立存在，但是有其主语部分和谓语部分，外观上像一个完整的句子。与主句的不同之处在于从句须由一个关联词（Connective）引导。

根据在句子中的成分和功能作用，复合句可分为名词性从句（主语从句、宾语从句、表语从句和同位语从句）、定语从句（形容词性从句）和状语从句（副词性从句）。

例如：

<u>The foreigners took a lot of pictures</u> when they were visiting the Great Wall.
　　（Principal Clause）　　　　　　（Adverbial Clause of Time）

二、英语句子的写作要素

英语句子具备四大要素——连贯性、一致性、简洁性和多样性，换句话说，即句法正确、逻辑严密、简洁明确和注重修辞。

（一）连贯性

连贯性是指句子各部分之间具有合理、清楚的联系。不连贯的句子通常表现在以下几个方面：人称、数、时态、语态混乱，代词指代不清，平行结构使用错误，修饰语与被修饰部分的关系不明确等。

例1：An important thing for the student to keep in mind is that when taking an exam, you should not cheat.

应改为：An important thing for the students to keep in mind is that when taking an exam, he/she should not cheat.

例2：Those who wish to see the film tonight are expected to obtain his ticket at noon.

应改为：Those who wish to see the film tonight are expected to obtain their tickets at noon.

例3：When the speaker entered the hall, the audiences stand up to greet him.

应改为：When the speaker entered the hall, the audience stood up to greet him.

例4：He memorized all the new words taught the day before and the composition assigned by his teacher was written.

应改为：He memorized all the new words taught the day before and wrote the composition assigned by his teacher.

分析：以上四个句子不够连贯，分别表现为人称、数、时态、语态四个方面的混乱。

例5：He told my brother that he was right.

应改为："I am right," he said to my brother.

或：He admitted that he was right and said so to my brother.

或："You are right," he said to my brother.

或：My brother was told that he was right.

例6：I will go to the lecture, for I like his poems.

应改为：I will go to the lecture, for I like the speaker's poems.

分析：以上两个例句中的代词指代不清。例 5 中第二个 he 既可以指主语，又可以指 my brother。例 6 中 his 究竟指代何人无从得知，所以换成名词所有格 the speaker's。

例 7：She said that she would come if she could, but not wait for her.

应改为：She said that she would come if she could, but we needn't wait for her.

例 8：Mr. Wang is energetic, capable and a man we can depend on.

应改为：Mr. Wang is an energetic and capable man (whom) we can depend on.

或：Mr. Wang is energetic and capable. We can depend on him.

分析：例 7 中 that she would come 与 not wait 不是平行结构，一个是从句，一个是不定式，应改后者为从句。例 8 也是平行结构使用错误。

例 9：She gave an excuse for not keeping her promise, that none of us believed.

应改为：She gave an excuse, that none of us believed, for not keeping her promise.

或：She gave an excuse for not keeping her promise, an excuse that none of us believed.

例 10：She almost finished reading 19 books at the weekend.

应改为：She finished reading almost 19 books at the weekend.

分析：例 9 和例 10 都属于修饰语错置的例子。例 9 中 that 从句修饰 promise，而实际上应该修饰 excuse。改进的办法是把这个从句移到 excuse 之后，或者重复使用一次 excuse。例 10 中的 almost 应该修饰 19 books 而不是 finish。

（二）一致性

一致性是指句子表达内容完整，逻辑关系紧密。前一种情况见例 11，后一种情况见例 12。

例 11：Lu Xun was one of the revolutionary writers.

应改为：Lu Xun was one of the Chinese revolutionary writers of the 20th century.

分析：该句意思不完整，国家和时期都没有提及。虽然鲁迅很有名气，但是外国人不是人人都知道他。

例 12：Mrs. Liu began to speak very fast at the meeting at 9 o'clock.

应改为：The meeting started at 9 o'clock and Mrs. Liu began to speak. She spoke very fast.

分析：该句逻辑关系不清晰，Mrs.Liu began to speak very fast 和 at 9 o'clock 之间有什么联系呢？显然缺少一致性。经修改后，原句扩展为两句，首先阐明时间关系，其次说明 Mrs.Liu 的讲话方式。

（三）简洁性

简洁性是指句中不应该有任何多余的词，只要充分、清晰地表达出意思，用词越少越好。

例 13：In my opinion, I think it is a good idea.

应改为：In my opinion, it is a good idea.

或：I think it is a good idea.

例 14：The book was jointly written by Professor Li in collaboration with some of his young students.

应改为：The book was jointly written by Professor Li and some of his young students.

或：The book was written by Professor Li in collaboration with some of his young students.

分析：上述两句中重复使用意思相同的词或短语，即 in my opinion 和 I think，jointly 与 in collaboration with。

为了获得简洁的效果，有时需要改变句子结构。

例 15：There are more and more people who come to realize the importance of mental health.

应改为：More and more people come to realize the importance of mental health.

例 16：Mr. Tang likes to drink all kinds of liquor that are produced in Hunan Province.

应改为：Mr.Tang prefers liquor produced in Hunan Province.

或：Mr.Tang prefers Hunan liquor.

分析：以上两句说明，可以通过合并主句与从句或者把从句压缩为短语或单词来获得简洁性。

（四）多样性

结构类似、长短相同、主语同一的句子频繁出现，必然令人乏味。因此，写作时要经常变换句型和句子结构，句式的多样性有助于取得较好的修辞效果。

例 17：I finished my homework and began to review the lessons.

应改为：Having finished my homework，1 began to review the lessons.

分析：用分词或分词短语开头，符合英文句子的表达习惯。

例 18：He was intelligent and hard-working, and he graduated with honors.

应改为：Intelligent and hard-working，he graduated with honors.

分析：用形容词引起句子，生动而活泼。

例 19：The girl was in despair and turned to her friends for help.

应改为：In despair, the girl turned to her friends for help.

分析：介词短语常常出现在英文句子开始部分。

例 20：He spoke slowly and emphatically to make everything clear.

应改为：To make everything clear, he spoke slowly and emphatically.

分析：不定式短语作目的状语，经常置于句首。

例 21：He worked hard day and night to pass the exams.

应改为：To pass the exams, he worked hard day and night.

分析：表示目的的不定式短语置于句首，可以起到强调作用。

【练习 1】修改下列各句，以符合句子写作要素。

① I heard the joke on the plane which did not amuse me at all.

② I lost some interesting books and found them a week later. My classmate had helped me.

③ I will attend the class, for I like her lecture.

④ Looking out of the window, a high mountain blocked my view.

⑤ His name is called James Bond.

⑥ Wherever he goes, he visits the places of interest there and misses none of them.

⑦ Liu was the student who was elected the monitor of the class by the whole class.

⑧ She is not only a famous singer, but also a super dancer as well.

⑨ Tom is earnest, responsible, honest, and a man you can trust.

⑩ He drank a cup of tea and a newspaper at the table was read.

三、常见表达错误实例分析

英语作文的表达错误往往属于"并发症",即一个句子同时出现几处不同类型的错误。纠正错误必须考虑上下文。以下列举、分析的是学生英语作文中常见的错句或病句,例句的一部分不符合英语的表达:

例1：A century years ago, there must be a lot of fish in this river.

［错误类型］表达多余、重复、时态错误

［修改参考］

(1) There must have been a lot of fish in this river a hundred years ago.

(2) There must have been a lot of fish in this river a century ago.

例2：Five decades years ago, we didn't know what is television.

［错误类型］表达多余、重复、逻辑错误、时态错误

［修改参考］

(1) Five decades ago, people didn't know what television was.

(2) Half a century ago, what television was remained unknown to people.

例3：We no need to tolerant dark at night due to the lights.

［错误类型］句子结构错误、词语用法错误、表达多余、重复、汉化表达错误

［修改参考］

(1) Humans don't have to tolerate dark thanks to the invention of the electric light.

（2）The invention of the electric light enabled people to be more productive.

例5：Science and technology has it's two faces. One is good for our life. But another is bad for our future.

［错误类型］词语用法错误、汉化表达错误

［修改参考］

（1）Science and technology has two sides: One is blessing, and the other is cursing.

（2）Science and technology functions positively and negatively to humans.

例6：Many years ago, there is no TV, people can only listen to the radio.

［错误类型］时态和语态错误、逻辑错误

［修改参考］

（1）Many years ago, people didn't know the radio or the TV.

（2）Many years ago, the TV and the radio were not known to people.

例7：In my view, the wrongdoer should not due to our science and technology.

［错误类型］句子结构错误、词语用法错误、汉化表达错误

［修改参考］

（1）In my view, science and technology is not the wrongdoer.

（2）I believe that this has nothing to do with science and technology.

例8：And the science and technology will good service for our mankind.

［错误类型］词语用法错误、汉化表达错误

［修改参考］

（1）And science and technology is expected to serve the mankind in a proper way.

（2）Human should make science and technology a good servant to humans.

例9：It delays our death.

［错误类型］词语用法错误、汉化表达错误、逻辑错误

［修改参考］

（1）It enables human beings to live a longer life.

（2）It prolonged human longevity.

例 10：Science and technology takes us good things, but also takes us bad things.

［错误类型］词语用法错误、表达多余、重复、汉化表达错误

［修改参考］

（1）Science and technology has not only done good but also harm to us.

（2）Science and technology is a double- edged sword.

例 11：Our lives have had a huge different.

［错误类型］词语用法错误、汉化表达错误

［修改参考］

（1）Our life is quite different from what it used to be.

（2）Our life takes on a different look.

例 12：The fridge for example, we can put the remain thing into it.

［错误类型］句子结构错误、词语用法错误、汉化表达错误、逻辑错误

［修改参考］

（1）The fridge, for example, can keep food fresh over a period in a cold temperature.

（2）For example, the fridge can preserve food in an ideal state for some time.

例 13：We can't progress if without science and technology.

［错误类型］句子结构错误、词语用法错误、汉化表达错误

［修改参考］

（1）Without science and technology, no progress would have been made.

（2）But for science and technology , man would not have enjoyed richness so much.

例 14：We become more and more rich and comfortable.

［错误类型］词语用法错误、汉化表达错误

［修改参考］

（1）People have become richer and richer, and human life is getting more and more comfortable.

（2）We are increasingly rich and comfortable.

例 15： Furthermore, more and more science and technology are used in army.

［错误类型］词语用法错误、汉化表达错误

［修改参考］

（1）Also, science and technology is more and more widely used in the military.

（2）Besides, science and technology is overused for military purposes.

例 16：I have never dreamed that I'll have a mobile telephone 10 years ago, but now it's come true!

［错误类型］时态和语态错误、词语用法错误、汉化表达错误、逻辑错误

［修改参考］

（1）I could hardly imagine having a mobile telephone 10 years ago, but now it turns out to be a reality.

（2）Having a mobile was a dream ten years ago but a common tool today for people.

例 17：It enable man to solve the problem as big as that economic development or as small as household's account-keeping.

［错误类型］词语用法错误、表达多余、重复、汉化表达错误

［修改参考］

（1）It enables man to solve problems as big as those concerning economic development or as small as those about household's account-keeping.

（2）It makes solving problems of various kinds–big or small–possible.

例 18：However, we are also suffering many problems from the development of science and technology.

［错误类型］词语用法错误、汉化表达错误

［修改参考］

（1）However, we are also confronting many problems arising from the development of science and technology.

（2）The development of science and technology, however, has brought about many problems to humans.

例 19：On the first hand ... on the second hand ...

［错误类型］词语用法错误、汉化表达错误

［修改参考］

（1）On the one hand .... on the other hand ...

（2）For one thing .... for another thing ...

例 20. Our life level raise to a high level.

［错误类型］句子结构错误、词语用法错误、汉化表达错误

［修改参考］

（1）Our life has been improved to a higher level.

（2）Living conditions are much better than ever before.

【练习 2】改正下列句子中的错误。

Exercise One（主谓一致）

① The police is looking for the escaped prisoner.

② The number of girl students in the English Department are great.

③ A number of foreigner scholars was invited to the anniversary celebration of our university.

④ Nowadays news are translated instantly to mass audiences.

⑤ Physics are taught by a Mr. Smith.

Exercise Two（代词和先行词一致）

① Either Bill or John will bring a sample of their own work.

② Jane and Jill called her friend.

③ Either Mary or her friends will present her design.

④ Every employee wants to impress his or her employer.

⑤ Each of the boys had their homework finished.

Exercise Three（句式混乱导致主题不鲜明）

① A lifetime is short, but much can be accomplished.

② In spite of the fact that she became a great professor, Jane Martin had a speech defect.

③ When most drivers apply the brakes, they are in doubt.

④ Corruption in high places became widespread; the government was considerably weakened.

⑤ Gary took a shower, and he thought of a great idea.

⑥ Mr. Martin left his office early. Nobody knew why he did.

⑦ The final examination was easy, but he passed with a low grade.

⑧ Our biology professor has written a book; it has a bright-red cover.

Exercise Four（统一性和连贯性）

① It rained heavily at 9 o'clock.

② Shakespeare was one of the greatest dramatists.

③ Many people believe that one should eat garlic everyday to prevent disease in that region.

④ The soil erosion only damaged a few houses.

⑤ Instead of taking physics, chemistry was chosen by most students in our class.

Exercise Five（句式呆板）

① The gardener who had cut the weeds thought about the vacation planned for August.

② When they saw the curtain go up, the audience gasped in surprise and started applauding loudly.

③ The man was looking forward to living an easy life in Canada after he had amassed a fortune.

④ She hurried down to the bank, withdrew all her savings, and gave them to her mother.

⑤ The new recruits lined up rapidly and the officers gave them their orders for the day.

第二节 段落写作

一、段落的组成

写作首先是段落写作。一篇文章可能由几个到十几个甚至更多的段落组成。因此，段落写作的成功与否直接关系到整篇文章的好坏。段落一般由若干句子组成，但从功能来说，尤其是说明文、论述文，段落里面的句子只有两类：主题句和支持句。

英语段落和汉语段落有所不同。它既是全文的一个组成部分，又自成一体，有相对独立的主题思想。为了能使这个主题思想得到阐述和发展，英语段落往往用一个句子来概括这个主题，并置于段落中的显著位置，如段首或段尾等，这个句子就被称为主题句（topic sentence）。段落内的其他句子都围绕其展开，对其进行叙述、说明或论证，这些句子被称为支持句（supporting sentences）。在英语的说明文、议论文中，"主题句＋支持句"的英语段落占60%~70%以上。较长的段落，在结尾还有结尾句（concluding sentence），通过归纳和主题句形成首尾呼应，有时还同时起到引出下一个段落的作用。

二、段落写作方法

（一）时间顺序

时间顺序法是指按事件发生的先后顺序发展段落，即首先发生的事情放在第一，最后发生的事情列在最后。这种方法主要在记叙文中使用，叙述事件的发展过程，谓语动词经常用过去时态，也可用于说明文，用于叙述程序或步骤。

常用的按时间顺序扩展段落的写作技巧为以下三种：

第一，首先要确定主题和主题句；

第二，按时间顺序交代事情的经过或程序；

第三，为使段落之间衔接更加连贯，可适当使用一些表示时间或顺序的过渡词，例如：

① at the beginning, after that, then, finally 等;

② first, then, next, in the end 等;

③ at first, later, after a while, afterwards, eventually 等。

[范例1]

The Statue of Liberty was a gift to the United States in the nineteenth century from the people of France in memory of the victory of the American Independent War. The statue was designed by the sculptor Auguste Bartholdi and the metal framework had been constructed by Gustave Eiffel. Construction of the statue began in France in the year of 1875, and it took ten years to complete. Before it was transported to the United States, a pedestal was built on Elis Island at the entrance of New York Harbor. The pedestal was designed by architect Richard M.Hunt in 1877. Construction of the pedestal began in 1883 and was completed in 1884, and final assembly of the statue and pedestal was completed in 1886. On October 28, 1886 President Grover Cleveland accepted the statue on behalf of the United States. Ever since then, the great monument has become the recognized symbol of liberty throughout the world.

[范文评析] 这一段文字用时间顺序法交代了自由女神像的制作过程。为了纪念美国独立战争的胜利,法国建造了自由女神像作为礼物送给美国。自由女神像从1875年在法国开始建造,历时10年完工。自由女神像的基座于1883年开始建造,1884年建成。1886年完成自由女神像和基座的衔接。1886年10月28日,美国总统格罗弗·克利夫兰代表美国人民接受了法国人民的礼物。从那以后,自由女神像成为世界公认的自由的象征。

(二) 空间扩展

当我们描述事物时,往往根据其所在地点及相互关系来扩展段落。这种方法主要用于描写文和记叙文。

按空间顺序扩展段落的写作技巧为以下两点:

第一,要有一个参照点,如上下、前后、左右、内外、远近等;

第二,使用一些表示空间顺序的过渡词,如 above—under, up—down, over—

below、on top of—at the bottom of、before—behind、on the left—on the right、in front of—at the back of、far—near、outside—inside、exterior—interior、in the middle of、in the center of、against、between、beside、beyond、across、farther、close to、next to、opposite to 等。

[范例1]

Completed in September 1993 and opened in October, the Yangpu Bridge is located in the downtown area, Shanghai. The Yangpu Bridge is among the world's longest bridges, with a total length of 8,354 meters. Its longest span of 602 meters makes it the fourth largest cable-stayed bridge in the world. It is a double-tower and double-cable-stayed bridge, with the bridge proper (the part that spans the river) 1,172 meters long. Its 30.35-meter width has altogether six lanes of traffic (3 for each direction). Its two pylons reach 223 meters in height. The highest ship clearance height—the distance between the river below, at normal water levels, and the underside of the bridge above is 48 meters, a necessity due to the heavy river traffic.

[范文评析] 这段文字按"长—宽—高"的空间顺序描述了杨浦大桥。

(三) 因果关系

因果关系用于解释事情发生的原因和结果，常用于说明文或议论文中。

常见的因果关系写作技巧有以下三种：

第一，先陈述结果，分析产生该结果的原因，或者先陈述原因，然后分析其引起的结果；

第二，着重分析直接的、明显的原因；

第三，使用一些表示原因和结果的过渡词，例如：

①表示原因：because、because of、due to、owing to、since、as、on account of、result from 等；

②表示结果：therefore、accordingly、consequently、as a result、contribute to、for this reason、lead to、result in 等。

（四）分类法

分类法按一定标准对事物进行归类。通过分类，使文章脉络一目了然。

常见的分类法写作技巧为以下两点：

第一，分类标准要统一，要完整周密，不能交错重叠；

第二，用一些表示分类的过渡词语，可以使分类及所分条目一目了然，例如：to distinguish, to divide ... into ... , to classify ... into ... , to fall into 等；kinds, types, sorts, groups, categories 等；according to, in terms of, depending on, on the basis of 等；to sub-classify, to sub-categorize, to sub-divide 等。

［范例1］

Studies serve for delight, for ornament, and for ability. Their chief use for delight, is in privateness and retiring; for ornament, is in discourse; and for ability, is in the judgment, and disposition of business.

［范文评析］培根把读书的境界分为三种：怡情、博彩、长才。

三、段落写作练习

【练习1】

1. 利用下列内容按照时间顺序就 Father's Day 写一个段落。

a. Father's Day was invented by Sonora Smart Dodd, to honor her father.

b. The first Father's Day was celebrated on June 19, 1910.

c. In 1924 President Calvin Coolidge supported the idea of a national Father's Day.

d. In 1966 President Lyndon Johnson signed a presidential proclamation declaring the third Sunday of June as Father's Day.

2. 按空间拓展方法写一段话描述你住的房屋或宿舍。利用下面提供的主题句：

The apartment/dormitory I live in ...

3. 根据下面的主题句，利用因果方法写一个段落。

Traffic accident is one of human beings' fatal enemies. The major cause for traffic accidents is the lack of safety awareness. Therefore ...

4. 根据下面的主题句，利用分类法写一个段落。

Love is of three varieties: unselfish, mutual and selfish ...

第三节　篇章写作

一、记叙文

（一）记叙文概述

记叙文，又称叙述文或记事文，是按照时间顺序叙述人物的经历和事情的产生、发展和变化过程的文章。具体而言，记叙文有故事、传记、游记、历史文献、新闻报道等形式。记叙文是最常见和应用最广泛的一种文体，同时又是进行其他各类文章写作的基础，如描写文、议论文、说明文等都有记叙的成分。作者写记叙文时目的必须明确，取材、结构、细节都应精心设计，以突出主题。因此，记叙文的写作练习是一项重要的基本功训练。

（二）记叙文写作要领

1. 明确中心思想

记叙类文章必须要有中心思想，文中的一切内容均应自始至终围绕中心展开。

2. 包含六个要素

记叙文通常包含六个要素，即所叙述事情的时间、地点、人物、事件、原因及结果。写作时应尽量将六个要素交代清楚，使读者了解事件的来龙去脉。

3. 使用恰当的叙事方式

记叙文的写作要安排好结构，选择合适的叙述方式。叙事的方法有顺叙、倒叙、插叙和夹叙夹议等。顺叙（in sequence of time）是指按事件发生、发展的先后顺序进行叙述。倒叙（flashback）则是把事件的结局提到前面叙述，然后再按事件的进展顺序进行叙述。插叙（narration interspersed with flashbacks）是在叙述过程中，由于某种需要，暂时把叙述的线索中断，插入与之相关的另外一件事。夹叙夹议（narration interspersed with comments）则是一面叙述事情，一面对这件事情加以分析或评论。顺叙是英语写作中最常用的叙述方式，有时也采用倒叙、插叙或夹叙夹议的手法。

4. 注意时态的一致

记叙文常用过去时态，即大多使用一般过去时、过去完成时、过去进行时和过去将来时。叙事时以一般过去时为主，必要时还会用到其他过去时态。例如，在倒叙时要用过去完成时，在描述某个具体情节时要用过去进行时，在谈及未来时则要用过去将来时等。

5. 注意人称的一致

人称是记叙文进行叙述的"基准点"，记叙中的主体都要用人称来表示，记叙文基本采用第一人称或第三人称作为叙述的主体。人称应通篇保持一致，除非特殊需要，一般不可在行文中更换人称。

6. 选择细节，叙事详略得当

记叙文涉及的细节均要利于表现主题，主题要明确，切勿不加选择地罗列所有相关内容，把文章写成"流水账"，而应有目的地将有意义、有价值的重要事件呈现给读者。因此，写作时应围绕主题思想精心设计情节，主要情节要详述，次要情节要略写甚至省去。

7. 注意对话的运用

记叙文中对话的使用也很重要，从对话中既能了解事情的变化，也可间接衬托出说话者的个性与见解。需要注意的是，对话须使用有代表性的语句，且须紧扣主题。

（三）记叙文范例与赏析

［范例1］

An Adventure

One sunny morning in summer I left my sister's house and went for a walk along a hilly path. It was a warm day and there was on one on the path. At the end of the path

I was sitting down to rest when a big black dog suddenly appeared. It ran up to me barking and lay down at my feet. I touched its head. When I started to walk home, it followed me and it would not go away. It had a collar round its neck but there was no name on the collar. When I got home, I rang up the nearest police station. I told the police that I had found a big black dog. I said that I would keep it until its owner called for it. I gave the police my name and address. Two days later an old gentleman came to my home to ask about the dog. He said he had lost his dog because it hated riding in cars One day it jumped out of the open window of his car. He offered me ten dollars, but I did not take the money. Then he game me his name and address and invited me to visit him.

［赏析］本文是一篇以第一人称写作的记叙文。记叙文写作时视角的掌握非常重要，用第一人称的视角叙述，主观色彩较浓，显得真切，便于表达细腻的思想感情。这种形式常用于写自传、本人经历或记叙耳闻目睹的事件。本文作者以第一人称的形式叙述自己在夏天一个早晨的经历，主题鲜明，行文流畅，表达清晰。文章第一句 One sunny morning in summer I left my sister's house and went for a walk along a hilly path 交代了人物、事件、时间和地点四个要素，之后按照时间的先后顺序进行叙述：从早晨离开姐姐家去散步，坐下来休息，到狗的出现，然后到家给警察局打电话……在时态方面，本文使用的是典型的记叙文常用时态。

（四）记叙文常用句型

1. 记叙文开头常用句型

（1）A little over... years ago, someone began doing something...

（2）After a couple of years of doing something, I have discovered...

（3）Upon graduation from... I went to work in...

（4）We began our (activity/job/work) on (month/date/year) ...

（5）While I was doing something, I saw...advertised in (a newspaper/a magazine/on TV).

（6）At the age of... someone did something/something occurred to someone...

（7） I had no idea of what lay in store for me the first time I walked into...

（8） It was a warm/hot/cold day in (some year), someone was doing something...

（9） Before someone did something, he/ she had done something else...

（10） I was... years old when something happened...

（11） I had only once done something. It happened in (a certain month) some year ago.

2. 记叙文过渡段落常用句型

（1） As fate would have it...

（2） What is worse is that...

（3） A very similar story can be told from...

（4） The case is only one example of...

（5） While everybody was rejoicing a... things took an abrupt change.

3. 记叙文结尾常用句型

（1） Whenever I recall... I cannot help thinking...

（2） Seeing/ Hearing... was the most... that 1...

（3） There is no such thing as an endless tale, is there? Likewise my narration has to come to an end now. And the last words I would like to add to my narration are that...

（4） It can be safely said that a variety of morals can be drawn from such a misfortune as narrated above.

（5） The tale may not be true, but its underlying moral is significant...

【练习1】按要求完成下列写作练习。

Write about a farewell party or an occasion of reunion you have experienced in 120-150 words.

（1） List several occasions of farewell-bidding and reunion you have experienced in the first place, and then choose one of them as the subject of your piece.

（2）Recall what exactly happened on the occasion and your feelings towards the occasion.

（3）Write down what you have recalled in detail.

二、描写文

（一）描写文概述

描写文是根据人的感官或视觉等方面的印象用语言文字的形式对某一事物、事件、人物和场景进行详尽的描述。

第一，人物描写：人物的外貌、性格特征、心理活动、思想感情等。

第二，事物描写：事物的大小、形状、质地、功能、颜色、气味等。

第三，环境描写：地点的位置、周围环境等。

描写人物时，往往从外表入手，包括人的面部表情、举手投足等，还应通过人物的言语、行动或对待他人的态度来揭示人物的性格特征和思想感情。

描写场所、景物时，可按空间顺序，由近及远或由远及近、由中心向四周或由四周向中心，也可以按时间顺序写。人们描写场所往往是为了反映某地本身，但也可能是为了表现人物的性格特征或是营造某种气氛。

描写物品时，要依靠感官来描写其大小形状、质地、功能、颜色、气味等。

（二）描写文的基本模式

描写文一般可以分为三段：第一段引出描述的对象，第二段对描述对象进行详细描述，第三段归纳或感想。

（三）描写文范例与赏析

The Earliest Coins in China

Of the various currencies used in ancient China, the round bronze coin with a square hole in the center was by far the most common. The earliest coins in this form, known as Qin Ban Liang, were products of China's first centralized kingdom, the Qin dynasty, established by Qin Shi Huang in 221 B.C. Before the Qin dynasty, Chinese currency had taken many forms. Coins shaped like various items of clothing, farm implements or knives were in circulation, but they were costly and hard to produce and difficult to carry and transport. The new coins were a great improvement—they were relatively simple to cast and could be strung together for ease of transportation. The new coins also had a particular philosophical significance to the ancient Chinese, who made the coins to symbolize their belief that heaven was round and the earth was square, and that heaven sheltered the earth and all things in the universe were united. This concept of unity was important to the Qin emperors. who ruled over a unified China and believed their power great enough to spread to the four corners of the earth.

[赏析] 本文为描写事物的文章。描写事物应抓住其细节特征，做到层次分明，且通常须提及其形状、大小、颜色、质地、气味等。如果该物有实用价值，则须说明其用途及如何使用；如果该物与某人有关，则须叙述它在此人生活中的作用。不过，文章写作时我们应强调该物最为突出的特征。本文讲述的是中国货币发展过程中具有里程碑意义的"秦半两"，作者在描述其形状和制作材料时，强调了"秦半两"的造型象征着古代天圆地方的宇宙观这一重要特色。

（四）描写文常用句型

1. 描写文开头常用句型

（1）My grandpa is very old. His face is winked and his hair is quite white; but his eyes are like two stars...

（2）... is an ordinary woman like millions of... in China. She is unknown to the public, but...make her uncommon.

（3）Autumn is the most beautiful season in the year.

（4）Paddy, the youngest of the four, was fifteen.

（5）Today he/ she looked ten years younger.

（6）Hangzhou a region of rivers and lakes—is located at...

2. 描写文过渡段落常用句型

（1）On my way to...

（2）As time went by...

（3）Across the street from our apartment...

（4）In the center of the excited crowd...

（5）Walking along the banks and looking at the rippling Xiangjiang River...

（6）Looking out to the north from my flat, I could see...

【练习2】按要求完成下列写作练习。

Compose a short description about the season you like most in 120-150 words. Try to write vividly so that your writing can evoke an echo from the reader.

三、议论文

（一）议论文概述

议论文是一种既常见又十分重要的文体，在作文考试中运用得最多。议论文是一种以摆事实、讲道理为主的文体，依据一定的客观事实和逻辑推理，证明或者反驳一定的见解或主张。议论文通常围绕着某一个有争议的观点展开论证，陈述各种理由，表明作者立场，阐明作者观点看法。因此，在写作中要明确地表明赞成什么、反对什么，用词不能模棱两可，必须明确肯定。

议论文一般由论点、论据、论证三个基本要素组成。论点是指作者对于事物或者事件的基本观点，论据就是用来证明作者论点的材料和根据，论证是指运用论据来证明论点的过程。其中论点要鲜明，论据要合理、恰当、充分，论证过程要逻辑严密。论证方法总的来说包括两种：立论和驳论，所谓立论就是从正面来阐明观点，并用充分的证据来证明其正确性；驳论则是通过否定错误或意见，从而确立自己认为正确的论点。

（二）议论文写作要点

1. 论点明确

论点要明确，不要空洞、含糊或泛泛而谈。立论要有新意，使读者耳目一新，并从中得到启发。

2. 论据有力

论据要有说服力。首先，作者必须具有充足而有效的论据。经常用到的论据有具体事例、统计数据、来自权威人士的信息、真理、定律等。其次，论据的排列通常按照重要性递增，即按"次重要→重要"的顺序进行，并通过使用恰当的逻辑过渡语来表明各点之间的相对关系。

3. 论证严密

最常用的论证方法是逻辑推导法。逻辑法包含归纳法和演绎法两种：前者是指从特殊到一般，即从具体事例中归纳出某个结论；后者是指从一般到特殊，即从一般原理出发，通过对具体事例的分析得出某个特殊的结论。其他常用的论证方法有因果法、举例法、比较对照法和定义法等。议论文有时还用到驳论的方法，即驳斥对方论据的虚伪性或揭露对方论证中的谬误，从而推翻对方的观点，建立自己的新观点。立论常常和驳论交替使用，"立中有驳、驳中有立"，在论证自己观点的同时去驳斥、否定对方的观点。

4. 句式工整、语言规范

议论文较多使用逻辑严密的主从句，少用或不用省略句。在时态上，议论文与说明文相似，较多使用一般时态，包括一般现在时、现在进行时和现在完成时。

（三）议论文范例与赏析

My Views on Space Research

I cannot agree to the statement that money spent on space travel is wasted. On the contrary, I feel that space research does bring mankind real benefits.

First of all, there are all sorts of by-products of space research. Space research has improved the quality of life in all sorts of areas which do not seem to be directly concerned with space. Thanks to space research, we have, for example, better medicines, better technology in the kitchen and the office.

Furthermore, it is exciting for people to think of space travel. It is thrilling not only for small boys but also for adults to think of exploring the stars. It seems to meet some needs in the human spirit for adventure. Throughout history, man has aspired to go out to seek the unknown.Most corners of the earth have now been discovered and so we are turning our sights even farther afield.

Moreover, who knows when we will actually have a real need of space? The world is steadily becoming more and more over-populated. In addition, the resources of the world are being gradually used up. We may find that our children actually have to make use of any living-space and resources that can be found in space.

For these three reasons given above, I feel quite strongly that money spent on space research is money put to good use.

［赏析］本文是一篇比较典型的议论文。文章主题突出，层次清晰，逻辑性强，具有思辨性。对于 space research 这一话题，作者开篇即态度鲜明地提出了个人观点：space research does bring mankind real benefits（太空研究为人类带来真实的利益），立论清楚。主体论证分为三个次主题，每个次主题自成一段，分别由起承过渡词 first of all、furthermore、moreover 引领，并用"摆事实，讲道理"的方法逐一论证。

文章第二段用实例说明太空研究的副产品改善了我们的生活质量。第三段论证说明太空旅行可以满足人类探险精神的需要。第四段段首以疑问句 who knows... 激发读者兴趣，后文则站在前瞻角度说明随着世界人口的膨胀，生存资源逐渐被耗竭，或许真的有一天我们需要利用到太空中发现的生活空间和资源。文章末段为结尾段，虽只有短短一句话，作者却铿锵有力地重申自己的观点，认为对太空研究的投资是值得的，与文章首段呼应，点题有力。

（四）议论文常用句型

1. 议论文开头常用句型

（1）Currently there is a growing concern that...

（2）Recently the issue of... has been brought to public concern.

（3）Currently there is a general attitude towards...

（4）Now it is universally acknowledged that... but I wonder whether...

（5）There is a public controversy nowadays over the issue of...

2. 议论文篇中常用句型

（1）概述不同观点，如下：

① There is no consensus among people as to the view of...

② People may have different views on...

③ Attitudes toward... vary from person to person.

（2）对比与反驳，如下：

① Undoubtedly, I side with the latter opinion...

② From my point of view, it is more reasonable to support the former opinion rather than the latter one.

③ The advantages of... outweigh any benefit we gained from...

（3）解决问题，如下：

① This phenomenon exists for quite a few reasons.

② Here are some suggestions for dealing with...

③ The feasible way to solve the problem is...

（4）解释说明，如下：

① The causes of... are as follows.

② This is a good case in point.

③ The most typical example is that...

3. 议论文结尾常用句型

（1）It is necessary that quick actions should be taken to bring the situation under control.

（2）In view of the seriousness of the problem, effective measures should be taken.

（3）There is no easy solution to the problem of... but... might be helpful.

（4）Taking into account all these factors, we may safely draw the conclusion that...

【练习3】按要求完成下列写作练习。

Write a composition on the title of "Opportunity and Success" with no less than

120 words. Your composition should be based on the following outline.

（1）Contingency（偶然性）of opportunity

（2）Relationship between opportunity and success

（3）Conclusion

四、说明文

（一）说明文概述

说明文是介绍客观事物、阐明事理，通过揭示概念来说明事物的特征、本质及其规律性，给人准确的科学知识或正确思想。说明文解说事物的特点、发展变化规律，分析前因后果，目的在于让读者获得必要的信息，对事物有较完整、明晰的了解和认识。说明文和议论文关系密切，但在写作目的和方法上两者仍有区别。说明文主要通过事实客观地解释或说明事物本身，重在给人介绍，让人明白；议论文则以事实、数据等为证据，表明主观见解，使读者信服或赞同某一观点。四级考试中的说明文更多采用"说明＋议论"形式。

说明文应该按照逻辑顺序进行说明，同时应该选择具体的特点和细节来说明。常用于说明文的方法有举例、定义、分类、比较和对比、因果等方法。所以，说明文的写作思路要围绕说明顺序、事物特点和细节来展开。

（二）说明文写作要点

1. 中心思想突出

全文集中一个问题，以此为中心，从不同侧面进行阐述。

2. 条理清楚、浑然一体

各段之间以及段落内部应层次分明，体现明显的逻辑联系。

3. 语言客观准确，文风朴实

语言简练、通俗易懂，避免使用过分夸张和华而不实的辞藻。

4. 使用恰当的段落写作方法

每个段落的写作方法通常不尽相同，主体部分的各段落写作方法主要取决于它们各自的功能以及所涉及的内容。英语说明文段落写作主要有六种方法，即定义法、例证法、比较对照法、分类法、因果分析法、过程分析法。在实际写作中，我们很少单独采用上述几种方法中的某一种，不少段落或文章的写作都综合使用几种不同的写作方法。

5. 采用适当的语言表达方式

多用现在时态，常包括一般现在时、现在进行时和现在完成时。在语态上，多用被动语态。

（三）说明文范例与赏析

如前所述，英语说明文段落写作方法主要有六种，即定义法、例证法、比较对照法、分类法、因果分析法、过程分析法。

（四）说明文常用句型

1. 说明文开头常用句型

（1）What's...

（2）The connection between... and... can be shown as follows...

2. 说明文解释说明常用句型

（1）There are... types/kinds/sorts/varieties of...

（2）... can be classified/divided/categorized/grouped, etc. into... types/kinds, etc. according to/ based on...

（3）Compared wit.... it rose from.... to... percent.

3. 说明文结尾常用句型

（1）In a word/ In brief/ In short/To sum up...

（2）It is evident that...

（3）These findings may be summarized as follows...

【练习4】按要求完成下列练习。

Suppose you are a student volunteer to welcome the foreign guests who are visiting your campus, you are required to write a welcome letter to give a brief introduction to your university in 120-150 words.

第四节 写作技巧

一、高分突破技法和策略

（一）对应法

由于四、六级写作多是提纲式写作，我们可根据中文提纲，采用对应法把文章写成三段。下文中这两例都是采用了对应写作方式，将中文提纲分别扩展成三段，三段之间相互衔接，构成一个完整的篇章：

［范例1］

Directions: For this part, you are allowed thirty minutes to write a short essay entitled Why Are There So Many Rural Laborers in Big Cities? You should write at least 120 words but no more than 180 words.

（1）近年来越来越多的农民工涌入大城市。

（2）产生这一社会现象的原因。

（3）我的看法。

Why Are There So Many Rural Laborers in Big Cities?

For a number of years, there has been a steady rise in the number of rural laborers who flood into big cities. Many men work on construction sites, while many women work as dishwashers in restaurants or babysitters for city dwellers. Three reasons, in my mind, can account for this social phenomenon.

First and foremost, the limited land can no longer produce enough crops for an ever-increasing rural population. In the second place, there are far more opportunities in big cities—rural laborers dream of earning money through hard work. Last but not least, many of them want to live permanently in big cities, because they admire the way of living there, and wish their children to receive good education.

I firmly believe that if we try our best to create a healthy social atmosphere, rural laborers will make greater contribution to our nation.

[范文评析] 范文首先指出大量农民工涌入大城市这一现象,并引出第二段所阐述的三个原因。首先,农村有限的土地不能满足日益增长的人口消费需求。其次,大城市有更多的工作机会。最后,农民工向往大城市的生活,想永远居住在大城市。末段总结指出,如果创造一个健康的社会环境,农民工就可以为国家做出更大的贡献。

(二) 调整法

尽管是提纲式写作,提纲所提示的只是文章所要包括的主要内容,却不是文章的结构模式,因此应根据英语文章的类型,重新组织和安排文章内容。

[范例 2]

Directions: For this part, you are allowed thirty minutes to write a short essay entitled Money. You should write at least 120 words but no more than 180 words.

(1) 钱对生活非常重要。

(2) 但是人们对钱的看法不一。

(3) 你的看法。

Money

What is money? To this question, different people hold different answers. Some think money is the source of happiness, while some regard it as the root of all evils. As far as I am concerned, they both have their reasons.

Those who consider money as the source of happiness argue that money means massive houses, beautiful clothes, or luxurious cars, and can enable them and their families to live comfortably. They even believe that money can bring power, friendship, and love. But due to the temptation of money, there are many people who become thieves, robbers, or murderers. It is also out of the greed for money that some officials forget their duty and cause enormous losses to the country, so some people think that money is the root of all evil and suggest that we keep away from money.

In fact, money is merely a medium of exchange. It may bring you happiness; it may lead you to a life of crime. Whether it is good or bad depends on how it is used.

[范文评析] 本文第一段以 What is money? 开头，随后把文章主要内容引出。在第二段作者根据提纲的要求，分别对人们的观点进行分析，交代了人们对金钱的两种态度。第三段阐述自己的观点。

二、谋篇布局

（一）谋篇布局1

第一，将提示的第一句作为文章的第一句。

第二，将提示的第二句展开成文章的中心段落。

第三，将提示的第三句作为第一段的最后一句。

第四，在结论段归纳概括，提出建议。

（二）谋篇布局2

第一，根据主题加引言段，在段尾提出自己的观点。

第二，将提示的第一句和第二句写成文章的中心段落。

第三，根据文章的叙述重点，总结全文，提出方法等。

（三）谋篇布局3

第一，将提示的第一句和第二句合为第一段，在段尾提出自己的观点。

第二，说明自己的理由。

第三，结论段总结全文。

（四）谋篇布局4

第一，将提示中的第一句作为第一段主题句，然后拓展开。

第二，将提示中的第二句作为第二段的主题句，拓展说明。

第三，将提示中的第三句拓展成第三段，注意与上面两段的照应，使其有总览全文的作用。

三、首尾段写作

根据四、六级写作的特点，一般首段和尾段都要自己补上，那么怎样才能写好首尾段呢？请注意以下的首尾段写作方式：

（一）首段的写作

1. 首段的写作方式

首先运用事实性信息、调查或故事等引出话题；其次导入主题；最后提出自己的观点，也就是文章的论点。

2. 首段开篇的常见方式

（1）谚语法

谚语一般为众人所熟悉，用谚语提出自己的观点也比较容易被读者所接受。

As the saying goes, "Money makes the mare go", but there are many things we can't buy with money, such as time and true love ...

（2）定义法

定义法是通过对文章中的关键词做一些简单或正面或反面的解释，限定其范围，这样比较有利于引出主题，如："Practice makes perfect" is an old saying. It tells us that it does not matter if we are clumsy at doing something. As long as we keep on trying and practicing, we will do a good job in the end.

（3）提问法

通过一个或一连串的提问，可以激发读者的兴趣，从而引出主题。

① Do you have many friends? Are they similar to you or different from you? Which kind of friends do you prefer?

② What is a good student? Different people may have different answers to this question.

（4）概括法

概括法是先总结文章内容所涉及的现状，然后引出主题。

In recent years, with the development of science and technology, the Internet has come into more and more homes and is playing a more and more important role in our work and daily life. It has become a must to us, but at the same time, the Internet has also brought with it a lot of problems.

（5）故事法

故事法指用简单有趣的故事激发读者的兴趣，从而提出自己的观点。

（6）引语法

此方法可用在文章的开篇或结尾段，如"Just as eating without liking harms the health, learning without interest harms the memory and can't be retained." From Vinci's words we can see how important it is to motivate the students in language learning.

（7）调查法

为了得到读者的认可，文章的开始可以引出调查数据等，借以提出文章主题。

（8）假设法

假设法是指通过假设提出一种选择，交代文章要涉及的问题，从而提出文章的主题。如 Suppose you were offered two jobs, one is highly-paid but rather demanding, the other is less demanding, but poorly-paid, which would you prefer ...

（9）综合法

在实际的写作中，可以将上述方法综合起来，没有必要局限于某一种方法。

（二）结论段的写作

结论一般采用概括总结、重述主题或提建议等方式。

1. 重述或总结主题

重述主题是指在结论处以另外一种表达方式重申主题，与首段内容相照应。

Families offer us warmth and care. Friends give us strength and horizon. They both help us understand the world as it is. Both of them are the dearest parts in our life.

2. 提出建议

Since postcards do us more harm than good, since we have many other ways to convey our feelings and promote our friendship, I hope everyone will take actions now to stop using postcards.

3. 概括总结

As we can see from the above, living in the suburb we can stay away from pollution, lead an easy leisure time, and needn't invest too much money, so I prefer living in the suburb to living in the city.

4. 引用名人名言

In particular, I enjoy what Francis Bacon said "Studies serve for delight, for ornament and for ability."

5. 综合法

与首段一样，结论段也可以是多种方法的综合。一般说来，总结加建议的比较多。

第四章 英语语法学习策略与指导

在近年的大学英语四、六级统考中,对英语语法的考核并不拘泥于四选一的语法题,而是渗透于整张试卷之中。大学英语四、六级统考中的听力、完形填空、阅读理解都需要扎实的语法基础来分析句子的结构和整体意思,写作和翻译则更需要主动地运用语法规则来遣词造句。因此,学生必须认识到英语语法的重要性,认识到英语语法是一切考试和能力运用的基础而认真系统地对语法进行学习强化。本章节主要介绍了英语语法概述、语法的重点与难点、语法综合练习几个方面。

第一节 英语语法概述

一、英语句子成分

英语句子的成分可分为主要成分和附属成分。

(一)主要成分:主语、谓语、宾语、补足语

(1)主语

主语是谓语叙述的对象,主要由名词(包括名词化的形容词及名词短语)、代词、介词短语、不定式现在分词和名词性从句等担任。

The light in this room is poor.(名词)

The young are better fed today in many countries than ever before.(名词化的形容词)

The students of this school live in large dormitories.（名词短语）

They say prices are going to increase again.（代词）

From eight to twelve is my busiest time.（介词短语）

To cheat in examinations is punishable.（不定式）

Swimming is good for health.（现在分词）

That Shelley became a poet may have been due to his mother's influence.（名词性从句）

（2）谓语

谓语说明主语的动作、状态、性质或身份等，由动词担任。英语的谓语比较复杂，有时带有不同的情态动词或不同的时态或语态。例如：

We all desire happiness and health.

Most students in this class have learned English for six years.

（3）宾语

宾语表示动作的承受者。宾语的类型可分为：动词宾语和介词宾语两大类。

①动词宾语：可分为直接宾语、间接宾语、保留宾语、同源宾语、形式宾语和实际宾语等几种类型。担任动词宾语的词类或语法成分有：名词（含名词化的形容词）、代词、数词、不定式现在分词、名词性从句等。

They build a bridge near the village.（名词）

We should respect the old and cherish the young.（名词化的形容词）

I think I dropped something.（代词）

We need five.（数词）

The band began to play.（不定式）

They all avoid mentioning the name.（现在分词短语）

I wonder whether it's large enough.（名词性从句）

②介词宾语。担任介词宾语的词类有：名词、代词、介词、不定式现在分词、名词性从句等。

He is lying on the grass.

He bought a new watch for me.

（4）补足语

补足语分为宾语补足语和主语补足语。补足语是补充说明宾语和主语的语法成分，担任补足语的词类或语法成分有名词、代词、形容词、副词、介词短语、不定式、分词、名词性从句等。

①宾语补足语

They named the child Jack.

What do you think him?

②主语补足语（多位于连系动词之后或被动语态的句子中）

He proved an excellent student.

She looked tired but she was still cheerful.

（二）附属成分：状语、定语、同位语

（1）状语

状语修饰谓语动词、非限定动词、形容词、副词、介词短语或句子的语法成分。担任状语的词类或语法成分通常有副词、介词短语、名词、非限定动词和状语从句等。

She read slowly but distinctly.

Mend it with this glue.

（2）定语

定语描述或限制名词或代词的语法成分，可分为前置定语和后置定语两种。

①前置定语：通常由形容词、分词、名词担任，位于名词之前。

He is a diligent student.

After a satisfying meal you no longer feel hungry.

②后置定语：通常由形容词（短语）、介词短语、副词、不定式、分词、定语从句担任，位于名词之后。

The only person visible was a policeman.

They were not allowed time enough for sports and recreation.

（3）同位语

同位语在由两个或以上的语言单位构成的结构中，如果后一语言单位用以说明前者，而且它们具有相同的语法成分，这样的结构称为同位结构，后一语言单位就是前者的同位语。担任同位语的词类及结构有：名词、代词、数词、形容词和名词从句。

We <u>doctors</u> should be responsible for the patient.

They <u>each</u> excel in their respective fields.

二、英语短语的分类和语法功能

短语是介于句子和词汇之间的语言单位，短语对谓语动词或其他词类起修饰、限制、说明等语法作用。英语短语可分为：名词短语、形容词短语、介词短语、副词短语、动词短语、非限定动词短语等，它们可担任主语、谓语、宾语、定语、状语、补足语、同位语等语法成分。

（一）名词短语

名词短语具有主语、宾语、定语、补足语、状语、同位语的语法功能。

（1）<u>Psychology and economics</u> are social sciences.（主语）

（2）We missed <u>the start of the movie</u>.（宾语）

（二）形容词短语

形容词短语具有定语、补足语的语法功能。

（1）We came to a <u>very attractive</u> house.（定语）

（2）The classroom is <u>full of students</u>.（主语补足语）

（三）介词短语

介词短语具有后置定语、状语、宾语、补足语等语法功能。

（1）The man <u>behind the tree</u> may be our teacher.（后置定语）

（2）I go swimming every day <u>after work</u>.（状语）

（四）副词短语

副词短语具有状语的语法功能，常修饰动词、形容词、副词、介词短语、非限定动词或整个句子。

The teacher always explained his students' questions very patiently.

The wind blew pretty hard when we were on our way to the station.

（五）动词短语

动词短语通常在句中用作谓语。动词短语是由动词和其他词构成的短语，结构比较固定，在句中用作谓语，有不同的时态和语态。动词短语主要有如下几种：

（1）不及物动词 + 副词（无后续宾语）

How did this come about?

（2）不及物动词 + 介词（后续宾语）

We must abide by the rules of the game.

（3）及物动词 + 副词（宾语可位于副词前或副词后）

He let the team down by not trying hard enough.

（4）及物动词 + 宾语 + 介词（宾语位于动词之后）

She shut herself in her bedroom sobbing her heart out.

（5）动词 + 副词 + 介词（宾语位于介词之后）

I suppose I must put up with the loss.

（6）及物动词 + 名词 + 介词

这类动词短语的词义多取决于其中的名词词义。

You can make any use of it you like.（利用）

（六）非限定动词短语

非限定动词短语包括不定式短语、现在分词短语和过去分词短语，它们有以下语法功能：

第一，不定式短语：具有主语、宾语、补足语、定语、状语的语法功能。

① The most important purpose of first aid is to save someone's life.（主语补足语）

② Can you remind me to phone her tomorrow?（宾语补足语）

第二，现在分词短语：具有主语、宾语、补足语、定语、状语的语法功能。

① The sight of him set her heart beating fast.（宾语补足语）

② The road joining the villages is very narrow.（定语）

第三，过去分词短语：具有补足语、定语、状语的语法功能。

① I'm worried about how the money was spent.（主语补足语）

② She didn't want her daughter taken out after dark.（宾语补足语）

【练习1】

Ⅰ.确定下列各句中斜体部分的语法成分，以字母形式填入句末的括弧内。

A—主语，B—宾语，C—谓语动词，D—状语，E—宾语补足语，F—主语补足语，G—定语，H—同位语。

Model：His proposal is under consideration.（F）

1. There is nothing wrong with the watch.（   ）

2. His hobby is making model planes.（   ）

3. When the meeting will be held has not been announced.（   ）

4. You must get up very early to see the sunrise tomorrow morning.（   ）

5. So difficult is the problem that it cannot be solved without a computer.（   ）

6. He urged me to write a novel about love.（   ）

7. Don't forget to give my greetings to your parents.（   ）

Ⅱ.按下列各句的要求找出句中相应的语法成分。

1. People have thought about going into space for many years.

A. Predicate Verb：_____

B. Object：_____

2. Her parents left her to choose her own friends.

A. Object Complement：_____

B. Subject：_____

3. I found it impossible to solve all the problems with the time given.

A. Object：_____

B. Adverbial：_____

4. He had been compelled to give up much of his time to house work.

A. Predicate Verb：_____

B. Subject Complement：_____

Ⅲ．确定下列各句的句型，以字母形式填入句末括弧内。

A—SV，B—SVA，C—SVO，D—SVOA，E—SVOO，F—SVC，G—SVOC。

Model：I began to learn English three years ago.（D）

1. Many people consider the astronaut a great hero.（   ）

2. These oranges have kept fresh.（   ）

3. Did you leave the doors and windows firmly fastened?（   ）

4. The doctors seemed very capable.（   ）

5. This wool should make me a good thick sweater.（   ）

6. Iron rusts easily.（   ）

7. He shut the door with haste.（   ）

8. I said that he was a man of immense capacity.（   ）

第二节　语法的重点与难点

一、名词

（一）名词的复数

第一，一般在词尾直接加 s，如 book—books。

第二，以 -s、-x、-sh、-ch 结尾的名词，通常在词尾加 -es，如 bus—buses。

第三，以辅音字母加 -y 结尾的名词，把 -y 变为 i，再加 -es，如 baby—babies。（例外：部分专有名词直接加 s，Mary—Marys。）

第四，以 -f、-fe 结尾的名词，把 -f、-fe 变为 -v，再加 -es，如 knife—knives。（例外：roof—roofs，scarf—scarfs/scarves。）

第五，以 o 结尾的名词，有生命的加 es，无生命的加 s，如 tomato-tomatoes,

photo—photos。（例外：kangaroo—kangaroos, lingo—lingoes。）

第六，名词复数的不规则变化，如 man—men, woman—women, child—children, foot—feet, tooth—teeth, mouse—mice。

第七，单复数形式相同的名词，如 sheep（羊）等。

第八，表示"某国人"的名词遵循以下原则：中日不变，如 Chinese—Chinese, Japanese—Japanese；英法变，如 Englishman—Englishmen, Frenchman—Frenchmen；其他 s 加后面，如 American—Americans, German—Germans。

第九，只有复数形式的名词，如 trousers（裤子）, gasses（眼镜）, thanks（感谢）, clothes（衣服）。

第十，复合名词的变法，如 an apple tree—some apple trees, a girl student—some girl students。（例外：a woman teacher—some women teachers, a man teacher—some men teachers）

（二）名词的所有格

要表示名词的所有或其他关系时，名词采用所有格形式（The Possessive Case of Nouns）。名词的所有格分为两种：'s 所有格和 of 所有格。

1. 's 所有格一般用于有生命的名词

（1）单数名词词尾加 "'s"，复数名词词尾没有 s，也要加 "'s"。如：
the girl's room 这女孩的房间 children's books 儿童读物

（2）若名词已有复数词尾 s，只加 "'"。
the teachers' reading room 教师阅览室

（3）以 s 结尾的专有名词可加 "'s"，也可加 "'"，即 "s'" 但均读作 /iz/ 如：
Engels's/Engels' works 恩格斯的著作

（4）合成名词的所有格，在最后的一个名词的词尾加 "'s"。如：
the editor-in-chief's office 总编辑室

（5）如果某物为两人共有，则将最后一个名词变为所有格；如果表示各自的所有关系，则将两个名词都变成所有格。如：
① Kate and Mary's room 凯特和玛丽的房间（一间）

② Kate's and Mary's rooms 凯特的房间和玛丽的房间（两间）

2. 's 所有格使用对象

（1）一般说来，用于表示有生命的名词或视为有生命的名词。如：

Mr. Black's office 布莱克先生的办公室

a spider's web 蜘蛛网

（2）用于表示时间、距离、价格等的名词。如：

today's paper 今天的报纸

a stone's throw 一步之遥（很近）

（3）用于表示国家、城市、机关、团体等的名词。如：

the world's surface 地球表面

the majority's view 多数人的意见

（4）用于某些固定的词组中。如：

for heaven's sake/for God's sake 看在上帝的份儿上

the journey's end 路程尽头

3. 双重所有格

当 of 词组带有后置的 's 所有格时，该 of 所有格称为"双重所有格"。使用时应注意以下几点：

（1）双重所有格表示特指的某（些）人之所有，不能用于物或泛指的人。如：

two plays of Shakespeare's 莎士比亚的两部剧本

（2）可用 a、any、some 及数词等修饰 of 短语前的名词，但不能用 the。如：
亨利太太的每一个儿子都很受欢迎。

Any son of Mrs. Henry's is welcome.（√）

但是不能说：

The son of Mrs. Henry's is welcome.（×）

（3）可用 this、that、these 和 those 修饰 of 短语前面的名词，表示爱憎褒贬等情感。如：

this idea of Henry's 亨利的这一想法

that long face of Mary's 玛丽的那张长脸

二、冠词

（一）专有名词前冠词的用法

专有名词前一般不用冠词，如人名、地名前：Robert, Shakespeare, Washington, New York。

但也有以下特殊情况：

第一，在某些地理名词前要加定冠词，如江河、海洋、山脉、群岛、海峡海湾以及个别国家名称前。如：

the Thames River, the Pacific Ocean, the Himalayas, the Alps, the English Channel, the Persian Gulf, the Netherlands, the Philippines, the Vatican.

第二，由普通名词构成的专有名词（如一些国家、机构、团体、学校、报刊名称等）前大多要加定冠词。如：

the United States of America, the British Museum, the University of Utah, the People's Congress, the National Gallery, The People's Daily, The New York Times, The Washington Post, The Economist.

第三，以下专有名词前大多不使用冠词：

①车站、机场、广场、公园、街道、湖泊名称前

Central Station, Kennedy Airport, Times Square, Hyde Park, Riverside Avenue, Dongting Lake.

②节日名称前

National Day, New Year's Day, International Women's Day, Easter（复活节），Christmas.

③多数杂志名称和以专有名词起首的大学名称前

Time, New Scientist, Reader's Digest, Oxford University.

第四，人名前一般用零冠词，但指某一特定的人或表示某一个人时，可分别用定冠词和不定冠词。如：

The Robert you are looking for is in the library.

A Miss Johnson came to see you yesterday.

以上是专有名词前冠词的一般用法，还存在不少例外情况与人们的使用习惯有关系，这就需要学习者平时多加观察。

（二）抽象名词前冠词的用法

抽象名词前一般采用零冠词。如：

His plan ended in failure.

Honesty is the best policy.

当抽象名词表示某种特定的内容或被限制性较强的定语修饰时，常需要加定冠词。如：

Before the invention of gunpowder, men fought with bows and arrows.

I shall never forget the beauty of that lake.

当某些抽象名词带有修饰语，表示具体的"一种""一例""一次"等意义时，可加不定冠词。如：

Jealousy can be a destructive emotion.

The job demands someone with a college education.

三、代词

（一）人称代词

1. 分类

人称代词是表示"我""你""他""我们""你们""他们"等的词。人称代词有人称、数和格的变化。

英语的人称代词有三种人称：第一人称（First Person）指说话人自己；第二人称（Second Person）指说话的对方，即听话人；第三人称（Third Person）指谈论的对象。英语的三种人称又各有单、复数形式，还有主格（Subjective Case）和宾格（Objective Case）之分（表4-2-1）。

表 4-2-1 人称代词

人称格数	单数		复数	
	主格	宾格	主格	宾格
第一人称	I	me	we	us
第二人称	you	you	you	you
第三人称	he/she/it	him/her/it	they	them

2. 用法

第一，人称代词可以指人，也可以指物，在句子里可用作主语、宾语和表语。例如：

She majors in English. 她主修英语。（作主语）

Nothing could make me change my decision. 什么也不能使我改变决定。（作宾语）

If I were you, I'd go back immediately. 如果我是你，我会立刻回去。（作表语）

第二，以下为人称代词的一些特殊用法：

① we、you、they 可泛指一般人。例如：

We all make mistakes. 每个人都会犯错。

② she 除了指"她"外，还可以表示雌性动物、国家、船只、车辆等。例如：

This is my dog. She is four years old. 这是我的狗，它四岁了。

③并列人称代词的排列顺序：人称代词并列时，出于礼貌，第二、第三人称在前，第一人称在后。在表示不祥之事、承认错误或自我批评时，说话人一般把自己放在他人之前。例如：

You, he and I should help each other. 你、我还有他应互相帮助。

（二）物主代词

表示所有关系的代词，也可称为物主代词。物主代词分形容词性物主代词和名词性物主代词两种。

第一，物主代词既有表示所属的作用又有指代作用，例如：

John had cut his finger; apparently there was a broken glass on his desk. 约翰割破

了手指，显而易见，他桌子上有个破玻璃杯。

物主代词有形容词性（如 my、your 等）和名词性（如 mine、yours 等）两种，形容词性的物主代词属于限定词。名词性的物主代词在用法上相当于省略了中心名词的 -'s 属格结构，如 Jack's cap 意为 The cap is Jack's. His cap 意为 The cap is his。

第二，以下为名词性物主代词的句法功能：

①作主语，例如：

May I use your pen? Yours works better. 我可以用一用你的钢笔吗？你的比我的好用。

②作宾语，例如：

I love my motherland as much as you love yours. 我爱我的祖国就像你爱你的祖国一样深。

③作介词宾语，例如：

You should interpret what I said in my sense of the word, not in yours. 你应当按我所用的词义去解释我说的话，而不能按你自己的意义去解释。

④作主语补语，例如：

The life I have is yours, It's yours. It's yours. 我的生命属于你，属于你，属于你。

（三）指示代词

表示"那个""这个""这些""那些"等指示概念的代词。指示代词有 this、that、these、those 等，如 That is a good idea. 那是个好主意。

（四）自身代词

表示"我自己""你自己""他自己""我们自己""你们自己""他们自己"等的代词，也称为"反身代词"。如 She was talking to herself. 她自言自语。

反身代词的用法：反身代词表示主语发生的动作落在主语自己身上，或用来加强名词或代词的语气。

第一，作宾语：I hope he didn't hurt himself. She taught herself English.

第二，作同位语：You yourself said so. You can do it yourself.

第三，常与以下动词连用：hurt、dress、enjoy、say to、talk to、teach。

第四，还可以与介词连用：by oneself（靠自己，不需要别人帮忙），for oneself（替自己，为自己），to oneself（供自己用）。

（五）相互代词

表示相互关系的代词叫相互代词，有 each other 和 one another 两组，但从语法角度，这两组没什么区别。

（六）不定代词

不指明代替任何特定名词的代词叫不定代词。常见的不定代词有 each、every 等，以及含有 some-、any-、no 等的合成代词，如 anybody、something、no one。这些不定代词大都可以代替名词和形容词，在句中作主语、宾语、表语和定语，但 none 和由 some、any、no 等构成的复合不定代词只能作主语、宾语或表语；every 和 no 只能作定语。

1. other, another 的用法

两者均可指人，也可指物，other 意为"另外"，不确指，需要确指时前加定冠词 the，the other，意为 another "一个"。

（1）other

①后跟名词（单，复），泛指"别的，其他的"。

I'll go swimming with other friends tomorrow.

② the other 后跟名词单数或复数，或后不跟名词，特指两者中的另一个。

At last we got to the other side of the river.

③ others 后不加名词，泛指另外一些别的人或事物；the others 特指其余所有的人或事物。

Thirty in our class are girls, and the others are boys.

④泛指三者以上的"一些"不用加 the，用"some... others"的形式。

Some people like it, others not.

（2）another

泛指另一个，不与 the 连用，只能跟可数名词单数。

2. both, either, neither 的用法

他们均用于两者之间，neither、either 用作单数，both 用作复数。

（1）both：肯定句中表示"两者都"；用于否定句中表示"两者不都"，即部分否定。

Both of the sisters are good at English.

Both... and... 连接两个主语时，谓语动词用复数。

Both my bothers and I are teachers.

（2）neither：表示"两个都不"，either 表示"两个中的任何一个"，neither 是 either 的否定形式，词组 neither... nor... 是词组 either... or... 的否定形式，该词组作主语时谓语动词根据就近原则（Principle of Proximity）决定其形式，即谓语动词的单、复数形式取决于最靠近它的词语。例如：

Either you or he is right.

Neither he nor you are right.

（3）neither 是 both 的反义词，作形容词时与单数名词连用，不用 the。

Neither pen writes good. = Neither of the pens writes good.

（七）疑问代词

疑问代词有 who、whom、whose、what 和 which 等，在句子中用来构成特殊疑问句。疑问代词都可用作连接代词，引导名词性从句（主语从句、宾语从句和表语从句）。例如，Tell me who he is. 告诉我他是谁。

（八）关系代词

关系代词有 who、whom、whose、that、which、as 等。一方面，它们可用作引导从句的关联词，在定语从句中可作主语、表语宾语、定语等；另一方面，它们又代表主句中为定语从句所修饰的那个名词或代词（通称为先行词），如 He is the man whom you have been looking for. 他就是你要找的那个人。

四、形容词/副词

（一）形容词和副词比较级的形式和用法

1. as...as 结构

第一，两个事物或人进行比较，表示两者程度相等时，常用 as+ 形容词/副词原级 +as 的结构，表示"……样"，例如：

Mary is as clever as Linda. 玛丽和琳达一样聪明。

The airport was as crowded as ever. 机场还是像平常那样拥挤。

第二，这种结构的否定形式是 not as... as 和 not so... as，表示"不……那样"，例如：

It isn't so cold as yesterday. 今天不像昨天那样冷。（形容词）

Things are not as bad as you thought. 事情没有你想象得那么糟。

第三，as...as 结构的另一种模式是：as + many/much+ 名词 +as，例如：

Please take as many candies as you want. 想拿多少糖就拿多少糖。

第四，as...as 结构还有一种形式：as+ 形容词原级 + 名词词组 +as，例如：

This is not as interesting a book as that one. 这本书没有那本书有趣。

2. more...than 结构

第一，两个事物或人进行比较，常用 more...than 结构，即形容词/副词比较级 +than，表示两者在某方面的差异，例如：

She is taller than me. 她比我高。（形容词）

第二，这种结构的否定形式是 less...than，例如：

This purse is less expensive than that one. 这只钱包比那只便宜。（形容词）

第三，形容词和副词的比较级有时也可以单独使用，例如：

Could you speak more clearly? 你能不能讲清楚一点儿？（副词）

3. 形容词比较结构的一些其他用法

第一，more...than 结构除表示两个事物或人就同一方面进行比较外，还可以表示同一个事物或人本身在不同方面的比较，表示"与其……不如……而不是"，例如：

I'm more thirsty than hungry. 与其说我饿，不如说我渴。

more...than 结构的这一用法也适用于 less...than 的结构，意思正好相反。例如：

I'm less thirsty than hungry. 与其说我渴，不如说我饿。

第二，not more...than 表示"不如……"，no more...than 表示"和……一样不"（否定两者）。而与其相反，not less...than 表示"不如……不"，no less...than 表示"和……一样"（肯定两者）。比较下面几个句子的意思：

You are not more careful than Peter is. 你不如彼得仔细。

You are not less careful than Peter is. 你比彼得仔细（你不如彼得粗心）。

4. 副词比较结构的一些其他用法

more and more "越来越……"例如：

I like her more and more. 我越来越喜欢她了。

（二）形容词和副词最高级的形式和用法

第一，要对三个或三个以上的人或事物进行比较，就要用形容词或副词的最高级，其结构的基本形式是：(the) + 形容词/副词的最高级 + 比较范围，例如：

This is the largest city in Europe. 这是欧洲最大的城市。（形容词）

Of all the boys in the class, he jumps (the) highest. 在班上所有男生中他跳得最高。（副词）

第二，形容词的最高级有时也可单独使用，后面不跟比较的范围，例如：

You can take the fastest train to Shanghai. 你可以搭乘最快的火车去上海。

The oldest child is only seven. 最大的孩子才七岁。

I owe her the deepest gratitude. 我非常感激她。

第三，形容词的最高级有时会用状语 very、much、by far、far and away 来强调，例如：

This is the very greatest book. 这是本最棒的书。

He is by far the most active student in the class. 他是班上最活跃的学生。

五、动词

（一）现在完成时和现在完成进行时的区别

第一，在缺少丰富上下文的情况下，两种时态有时可互换，含义基本相同，如：

We have been living / have lived in this city for ten years.

They have been discussing / have discussed the problem for a long time.

第二，现在完成时明确表示动作的完成；现在完成进行时既可表示动作完成，也可表示动作尚未完成，有待继续，试比较：

I have written an article.（已写好）

I have been writing an article.（可能已写好，也可能还没完成，要继续写）

第三，现在完成时表示动作在说话前的过去某时业已完成；现在完成进行时则表示近期的动作，例如：

I have visited Japan.（表示说话前的过去某时已去过）

I have been visiting Japan.（表示近期的动作）

第四，表示次数的状语，如 twice/several times/many times 等只能与现在完成时连用，不可与现在完成进行时连用，因为现在完成进行时强调的是动作的持续，不能以次数来计算，如：

You have asked this question twice.（正）

You have been asking this question twice.（误）

（二）过去完成时与过去完成进行时的区别

第一，在缺少丰富上下文的情况下，两种时态有时可互换，含义基本相同，如：

I had been working for three hours when they came.

I had worked for three hours when they came.

第二，过去完成进行时强调动作的持续或可能完成，过去完成时则侧重动作的完成或结果，试比较：

She told me that she had cleaned the house.（已打扫完毕）

She said she had been cleaning the house.（可能尚未完成打扫）

By the end of last month, he had written altogether 15 novels.（强调动作的结果）

He had been writing novels all these years.（可能还在写作）

（三）现在完成时与一般过去时的区别

一般说来，一般过去时仅表示过去的动作或状态，与现在没有关系，现在完成时往往是为说明现在的情况，与现在有联系。试比较下列各对例子：

I lived in Shanghai for two years.（单纯表示过去的经历，现已不住上海了）

I have lived in Shanghai for two years.（表示现仍住上海）

He went to New York some years ago.（仅表示过去的经历，与现在没什么关系）

He has been to New York several times.（言外之意是：他现在已很熟悉纽约了）

（四）be going to+ 动词与 will+ 动词的区别

第一，表示"意愿"或"意图"时，be going to+ 动词指事先经过考虑的意图，而 will+ 动词则表示临时想到的打算，试比较：

She has bought some cloth. She is going to make herself a dress.

A：This is a terribly heavy box.

B：I'll help you to carry it.

第二，be going to+ 动词可用于条件状语从句中表示将来，will + 动词则不能，如：

If you are going to play tennis this afternoon, you'd better get your shoes changed.（句中画线部分不能用 will play 替代）

（五）be going to+ 动词与 be to+ 动词的区别

第一，be going to+ 动词表示现在打算将来要做的事情，be to+ 动词则表示按计划、安排即将发生的动作、计划或安排等。因此，be going to+ 动词不及 be to+ 动词正式。

I'm going to play tennis this afternoon.（表示一般的打算）

I'm to play tennis this afternoon.（表示按计划、安排的活动）

The president of an American university is to visit our school tomorrow.（表示按

计划的事宜，一般不会变动）

第二，be going to+ 动词可用于表示对将要发生的事件的预测或判断，因此主语可以是人或事；be to+ 动词则没有这种用法。如：

He is going to be fat.（不能说：He is to be fat.）

It is going to rain.（不能说：It is to rain.）

第三，be to+ 动词用于第二、第三人称可表示命令、禁止等情态意义，而 be going to+ 动词则没有这种用法。如：

You are not to smoke here.（不能说：You are not going to smoke here.）

（六）一般现在时与现在进行时表示将来时间的区别

一般现在时与现在进行时都可表示按计划、安排将要发生的动作，但前者表示按计划、安排的动作是不可改变或不可随便改变的，后者则没有那么严谨，试比较：

The train leaves at 7:30 this evening.（时刻表所规定，一般不可改变）

He is leaving tomorrow.（仅表示个人的安排，可随时变更）

六、介词

（一）动词和介词搭配

第一，不及物动词 + 介词，如：

He fell into the habit of excessive drinking. 他养成了酗酒的习惯。

常见的这一类短语有：

glance at 瞥见

grasp at 抓住

work at 致力于，从事

boast of 自夸

approve of 同意

account for 解释

stand for 赞同，支持

long for 期望

compete with 竞争

emerge from 出现，显露

recover from 恢复

confide in 信赖某人

intervene in 干涉，调停

stand by 支持

第二，及物动词＋宾语＋介词，如：

This photo reminds me of my childhood. 这张照片使我想起了我的童年。

The doctors are trying to prevent the disease from spreading. 医生们正努力防止疾病的蔓延。

常见的这一类短语有：

deprive sb. of sth. 剥夺，使丧失

relieve sb. of sth. 解除某人（负担，责任）

blame sb. for sth. 责备

persuade sb. of sth. 说服

accuse sb. of sth. 指控

excuse sb./sth. for sth. 宽恕

第三，动词＋副词＋介词，如：

She can't put up with his ridiculous idea. 她无法忍受他的荒唐想法。

His dishonesty will catch up with him one day. 总有一天，他的不诚实会给他带来麻烦。

常见的这一类短语有：

go in for 参加，选择……作职业

go through with 将……做到底

hold on to 保留

keep up with 跟上（形势）/ 和……保持联系

live up to 达到（期望），不辜负

make up for 补偿，弥补

第四，动词＋宾语＋副词＋介词，如：

These stories took me back to the age of innocence. 这些故事把我带回了纯真年代。

You should not take your resentment out on her. 你不应该怨恨她。

（二）一些形容词与不同介词构成固定搭配

Understanding and appreciating their history and culture will be critical to building a better world. 理解和尊重他们的历史和文化对建立一个更加美好的世界至关重要。

This umbrella is identical to the one my father has. 这把伞和我父亲的那把一模一样。

常见的这类短语有：

be curious about 好奇的

be mad at 对……生气

be annoyed about 生气的

be absent from 缺席的

be distinct from 分开的，不同的

be ready for 准备好

（三）名词和介词的搭配

He placed great emphasis on language study. 他非常重视语言学习。

This is the best solution to her financial troubles. 这是解决她经济困难的最好方法。

常见的这类搭配有：

about：complain, concern, opinion, doubt

between：difference, distinction, gap

from：separation, protection, relief, absence

for：anxiety, necessity, hope, affection, passion, request, desire, excuse, preference, explanation, reason, responsibility, application, apology, wish, reputation

in：belief, confidence, delight, difficulty, faith, improvement, proficiency

of：awareness, capability, innocence, ignorance, intention, lack

on：comment, concentration, effect, emphasis, impact, influence

to：access, appeal, approach, contribution, contrast, devotion, objection, obstacle, solution, response

with：association, connection, cooperation, contact, familiarity

第三节　语法综合练习

1. When I came in, I saw Dr. Lee _____ a patient.

A. examine　　　B. to examine　　　C. examining　　　D. examined

2. We object _____ punishing a whole class for one person's fault.

A. about　　　B. against　　　C. to　　　D. for

3. While _____ in Paris, the young lawyer picked up some French.

A. staying　　　B. to stay　　　C. stayed　　　D. stay

4. The machine will continue to make much noise _____ we have it repaired.

A. when　　　B. because　　　C. if　　　D. unless

5. _____ black clouds covering the sky, he stopped his work and went home.

A. To see　　　　　　　B. Having been seeing

C. Seeing　　　　　　　D. Having to see

6. It makes no difference to me _____ Mr. Smith will come or not.

A. when　　　B. whether　　　C. that　　　D. how

7. She has _____ her mind and is going to Canada instead of Japan.

A. exchange　　　B. changed　　　C. decided　　　D. made

8. Does he have difficulty _____ English?

A. to speak B. speak C. speaking D. spoke

9. In winter we go _____ on the hill.

A. skiing B. to ski C. ski D. for ski

10. She _____ playing volleyball very much.

A. has B. wants C. lets D. enjoys

11. The person _____ you were talking to was an American.

A. who B. whom C. which D. as

12. All _____ is a continuous supply of the basic necessities of life.

A. what is needed B. that is needed C. for our needs D. thing needed

13. The goals _____ he had fought all his life no longer seemed important to him.

A. for that B. for which C. for what D. of them

14. Snowdonia is a seashore city _____ you can enjoy yourselves much by visiting the local scenic spots.

A. why B. which C. where D. so

15. The inflation made it hard for us to buy the necessities _____.

A. which need us B. that we need C. what we need D. as we need

16. Those were the soldiers _____ responsibility was to save the town.

A. whose B. whom C. that D. from whom

17. _____ the population is too large, the government has to take measures to control the birth rate.

A. Although B. Since C. If D. Until

18. The fact _____ doctors recommend that children with hypertension(过度紧张) drink coffee is surprising.

A. what B. is that C. that D. of

19. I can never forget the day _____ I first came to college.

A. when B. in which C. at which D. which

20. I can never forget the day _____ we spent together.

A. when B. in which C. at which D. which

21. Young _____ he is, he knows what is the right thing to do.

A. that B. as C. although D. however

22. This novel is _____ the better of the two.

A. by far B. by too C. far too D. by the far

23. Do you feel like _____ a rest?

A. have B. to have C. had D. having

24. _____ he objected to your impolite behavior is quite understandable.

A. That B. what C. Which D. Whether

25. _____ he often forgot their wedding anniversary greatly annoyed his wife.

A. All B. What C. Which D. That

26. I don't care _____ or not she will apologize to me.

A. if B. whether C. what D. which

27. Seldom _____ any mistakes during my past five years of service here.

A. made I B. did I make C. should I make D. would I make

28. Not until the year of 1945 _____ made the capital of this province.

A. the city was B. was the city

C. when the city was D. was when the city

29. You will soon _____ this climate and then the changes in temperature will not affect you.

A. get used to B. get to C get over D. get on with

30. _____ is announced in the papers, a nation-wide sport meeting will be held in the city next month.

A. Because B. for C. As D. So

31. Do let your father know all the truth. He seems _____ everything.

A to have told B. having told

C. to have been told D. to be told

32. At the shopping center, she didn't know _____ and left with an empty bag.

A. what was to buy　　　　　　　　B. what to buy

C. which to buy　　　　　　　　　D. which to be bought

33. Smith is often heard _____ guitar every night in his room.

A. play　　　B. plays　　　C. playing　　　D. to play

34. The patient was warned _____ any hot food after the operation.

A. to eat not　　B. eating not　　C. not eating　　D. not to eat

35. Do remember _____ me a call when you arrive in Shanghai.

A. giving　　B. having given　　C. to give　　D. to have given

36. Jack is said _____ abroad now, but I don't know which country he is studying in.

A. having studied　　　　　　　B. to be studying

C. having been studied　　　　　D. to study

37. He entered the room quietly _____ wake up his family.

A. not so that　　B. so that not　　C. so as not to　　D. not so as to

38. He now regrets _____ harder when he was at school.

A. not to study　　　　　　　B. not studying

C. not having studied　　　　D. not to be studying

39. _____ his reply, Mary became very angry and decided to write again.

A. Not having received　　　　B. Having not received

C. Not received　　　　　　　D. Received not

40. The little girl, _____ her favorite doll, was crying loudly.

A. lost　　B. losing　　C. having lost　　D. had lost

41. The teacher had the naughty boy _____ for about an hour at the back of the classroom.

A. standing　　B. to stand　　C. stand　　D. stood

42. _____ a holiday, we went to the farm to help the farmers with their harvest.

A. being　　B. It being　　C. having been　　D. It was

43. After supper, many people stroll along the lake side, _____.

A. chatting and laughing　　　　B. to chat and to laugh

C. to chat and laugh　　　　　　D. chatted and laughed

44. It is reported that there had been a riot in the city, with thirty-five _____.

A. Injured　　B. injuring　　C. to be injured　　D. injure

45. The foreigner couldn't make himself _____ only by gesturing with his hands.

A understand　　　　　　　　B. understood

C. to be understood　　　　　　D. understanding

46. Though _____ in 1560s, the book still appeals to the readers today.

A. it written　　B. it was written　　C. written　　D. had written

47. I couldn't focus on the professor's lecture with all that noise _____.

A. going on　　B. goes on　　C. went on　　D. to go on

48. _____ in the queue for half an hour, Jack suddenly realized that he had left his wallet at home.

A. To wait　　B. Have waited　　C. Having waited　　D. To have waited

49. _____ the same treatment again, he is sure to recover from the operation.

A. Having give　　B. To give　　C. Giving　　D. Given

50. The experiment cannot be carried out because of _____.

A. the equipment is destroyed　　　　B. the equipment to be destroyed

C. the equipment being destroyed　　D. the equipment has been destroyed

第五章 英语翻译学习策略与指导

翻译不仅是外语教学与测试的重要手段,更是外语学习者应当掌握的语言技能。《大学英语教学大纲》(修订本)把培养学生一定的翻译能力明确列入教学目的之中,还对学生在"基础阶段"和"应用提高阶段"应当具备的翻译能力做出了定性和定量的要求。为了提升大学生英语翻译能力,本章分别介绍了翻译基本理论、中西思维差异、英语翻译常用技巧三方面内容。

第一节 翻译基本理论

一、翻译的标准

翻译标准是指导翻译实践的准则,是衡量译文质量的尺度。很久以来,翻译标准一直是翻译理论研究的重点课题,同时也是翻译工作者在实践中极为关注的重要问题。对于什么是科学合理、切实可行的翻译标准,译界始终是见仁见智、言人人殊,至今未有定论。围绕翻译标准的百家争鸣也从侧面上推动了翻译理论的发展,促进了翻译事业的繁荣。

在我国翻译史上,早在唐代,佛经翻译家玄奘就曾提出过"既须求真,又须喻俗"的翻译标准。所谓"求真"是指忠实于原文,"喻俗"则是指译文应当通顺易懂。清朝末年,严复在《天演论》卷首的译例言中提出了著名的"信、达、雅"三字翻译标准。在很多学者看来,严复所谓的"信""达"与玄奘提出的"求真""喻俗"实质上并无二致,应当看作是可以接受的两条标准,但他们对"雅"的看法却争议颇大。一种观点主张,不看原文的具体风格特征,一味追求译文的古雅是不足取的,因此,"雅"不能作为一条翻译标准:另一种观点则认为,假若赋予"雅"以新的含义,将其解释为译文要讲究修辞,译文要富于文采,那么"雅"仍不失为评价译文质量的一条标准。尽管翻译界对其认识不尽相同,但是在过去的一个世纪里严复的"信、达、雅"翻译标准一直被广泛引用和研究,其影响至今仍经久不衰。

当然,也有学者认为,早在严复前一个世纪,爱丁堡大学历史教授泰特勒(Alexander F.Tytler,1749—1814)就在《论翻译的原则》(Essay on the principles of Translation)中提出了翻译三原则,与严复的"信、达、雅"真可谓如出一辙。

(1) The translation should give a complete transcript of the ideas of the original work.

译文应完整地复述出原作的思想。

(2) The style and manner of writing should be of the same character as that of the original.

译文的风格和笔调应与原作的性质一致。

(3) The translation should have all the ease of the original composition.

译文应和原作一样流畅。

尽管人们对泰特勒的翻译三原则同对严复的"信、达、雅"翻译标准一样在理解上存在分歧,但很多有识之士认为,古今中外学者关于翻译标准的看法在本质上是基本一致的。虽然表述各异,却都将"准确流畅""通顺达意"看作翻译标准的要素。因此,目前翻译界倾向性的看法是主张以"忠实、通顺"作为翻译标准,这个四字标准言简意赅,尤其便于英汉翻译初学者理解和掌握,因而为许多英汉翻译教程广为采用。

所谓忠实,指的是译文必须完整准确地传达原作的思想内容,保持原作的语气和文体风格。这就要求译者一方面对原作叙述的事实、说明的道理、描写的景物以及所反映的作者的观点立场、思想情感等内容不妄加篡改、随意增删;另一方面又不以译者自己的风格取代原作的风格。原作的风格通常包括原作的民族风格、时代风格、语体风格以及作者个人的语言风格等。对于大学英语翻译课程的学习者而言,显然难以一步到位。因此,作为第一步,他们首先应当注意掌握不同语体（口语体与书面语体）和不同文体的特点及其对翻译的不同要求。

所谓通顺，指的是译文语言必须通畅易懂，遣词造句应当符合译语的语法规范和表达习惯，避免出现文理不通、逻辑不清、佶屈聱牙、晦涩难懂等现象。为此，切不可逐词死译、硬译。相反，应当在"忠实"的前提下，摆脱原文结构形式的束缚，按照译语的行文规范和表达习惯组织安排译文。只有这样，才能保证译文具有相应的可读性，避免译文变得洋腔洋调、生硬别扭。例如：

（1）It is now thought that the more work we give our brains, the more work they are able to do.

原译：现在被认为，我们给脑子的工作越多，它们能干的工作越多。

改译：现在人们认为，脑筋越用越灵活。

（2）The average shooting star is a small fragment of matter usually smaller than a pea and often no larger than a grain of sand.

原译：普通流星通常只是比豌豆还小，而且往往是并不比一粒沙子更大的物质碎片。

改译：普通流星是一种很小的物质碎片，通常比豌豆还小，只有沙粒那么大。

（3）Primarily the Allied task was to utilize the resources of two great nations with the decisiveness of single authority.

原译：盟国的任务主要是以统一领导的果断性来使用两个大国的资源。

改译：盟国的任务主要是在一个统一的领导下果断地使用两个大国的资源。

（4）Scientific discoveries and inventions do not always influence the language in proportion to their importance.

原译：科学的发现与发明，就其重要性的比例而言，并不总对语言有什么影响。

改译：科学发现和发明并不一定因其愈加重要而对语言的影响就愈大。

对比以上几例中的两种译文可以发现，"原译"大多拘泥于原文的表层形式，貌似忠实原文，实际上却使译文累赘费解，甚至有悖原义。这种译文显然违背了"忠实、通顺"的标准，而各例中的"改译"相比之下无疑更加自然晓畅、通顺达意，更加忠实于原文的含义。由此可见，虽然忠实与通顺有时似乎相互矛盾，但实质上是相辅相成的。忠实而不通顺，译文可读性差，读者无法理解，忠实也就无从谈起；通顺而不忠实，脱离原作的内容与风格，这样的译文也就称不上翻译，充其量只是一种编撰。因此，应当将"忠实、通顺"这一翻译标准看作统一的整体，二者不可偏废。

二、翻译过程

（一）理解

理解阶段的目的是全面领会原文作者所要表达的思想内容，不仅要弄清原文的字面意思和主要思想，还要透彻理解原文字里行间的深刻含义。本阶段主要包含以下两个步骤：

一是通读源语全文，宏观把握整篇文章的内容，真正读懂原文。正确理解句子间的逻辑关系，弄清代词的指代内容，为正确翻译出原文内容做好铺垫。

二是分析句子结构，透彻理解原文语句，这是正确翻译的关键。首先，应该找出句子的主干结构，确定句子的主语、谓语和宾语；其次，关注句子成分是否有省略、主句和从句之间的关系是否明确等语法问题。准确把握句子结构及其关系是保证译文语法正确、语言得当的重要环节。

（二）表达

表达指的是译者在译语中寻找恰当的词语，运用合适的方法和技巧将自己理解的原文内容加以转换的过程。表达得好坏取决于译者对原文的理解程度及其译语的素养和水平。理解是表达的基础，表达是理解的结果，由于两种语言代表两种完全不同的文化，其表达习惯也不尽相同，正确的理解并不一定会有正确的表达。因此，表达时需要灵活运用不同的翻译方法和技巧去行文措辞。"直译"和"意译"是两种最基本的翻译方法。

（三）校核

校核是复读原文及译文，进一步校对、核实、推敲、修改原文理解及译语表达的阶段，是前面两个阶段的深化。校核内容主要包括审查词语、句式及文本内容的翻译是否精准或存在错漏，是否有笔误、拼写错误等问题。校核是翻译过程中相当重要的一个阶段，通过校核，往往可以发现译文中存在的偏差，使译文更为完美流畅。

在这三个步骤中，理解和表达是两个关键环节，需要译者具备一定的能力和技巧。理解是表达的基础和前提，表达是源语理解及向译语转换的体现，没有准确的理解就没有顺畅的表达，二者不可分割。理解与表达是相互关联的过程，表达的过程中需要更深一步地理解原文。因此，汉英互译时，译者往往需要经历从英语到汉语，再从汉语到英语反复推敲的过程。

第二节　中西思维差异

一、整体与个体

"天人合一"是中国古人对自身与世界的认识。此概念最初可见《庄子·外篇·达生第十九》："天地者，万物父母也。合则成体，散则成始。"[1] 后经董仲舒的发展成为中国古典哲学的根本观念之一，并由此导致了中国人最基本思维结构"整体性"的诞生。具体表现在人们崇尚自身与周边世界的和谐，寻求整体统一。凡事先考虑整体，顾全大局。现今我们大力提倡构建和谐社会，实现人与自然、人与人、人与社会的和谐统一，即为一个很好的例证。

"天人相分"是古西方人对自身与世界的主流意识。西方文明发源于古希腊半岛。特殊的地理环境造就了航海业、手工业、商业等生活方式的萌芽与兴盛，也因此构建了与中国不同的人缘关系。西方人自古就重视个人利益，追求个人发展，偏重个体性的思维结构也因此产生。文艺复兴与宗教改革所推崇的个人主义就是最突出的表现。所以，西方人强调个体发展，重视个性的培养，追求先个体后整体、先局部后全部的发展模式。

地址翻译最能体现思维整体性和个体性的差异对翻译的影响。中国人的思维结构注重整体性，所以从大局着眼，在表述地址时总是把最高级别的地名放在首位，如中国湖南省长沙市天心区书院路37号竹园4号楼401室。

---

[1] 庄子.庄子[M].南昌：江西美术出版社，2018。

属于个体性思维结构的西方人则相反,把最小级别的地名放在首位,所以翻译时,得转换思维。故而,上述中文地址应译为 Room 401, Building 4 in Bamboo Garden, No. 37, Shuyuan Road, Tianxin District, Changsha, Hunan Province, China.

二、悟性与理性

悟性思维也叫直觉性思维,其重视实践经验,注重整体思考,因而借助直觉和感悟从总体上模糊而直接地把握认识对象的内在本质和规律。理性思维注重科学、理性、分析、实证,必须借助逻辑关系在论证推演中认识事物的本质和规律。汉民族的思维方式重悟性,英美民族则重理性。

(一)汉民族的悟性思维

对中国人思维方式影响最大的三种哲学——儒家、道家与中国佛教都非常重视悟性。悟性思维对中国的语言文化影响普遍而深远,在文学、绘画、医学、宗教等方面皆有诸多表现,在语言上的表现如下:

1. 汉语重悟性的突出表现是意合

意合的语言呈现出文字上的跳脱,特别是主语、代词和连词常常略去不提,但是,意念流仍然清晰,极少出现歧义。跳脱部分全凭"读者的悟性"去体味语句的内涵。如:

雨是最寻常的,(它)一下就是两三天。(不过)(你)可别恼。看,(它)(正在下着),(它)像花针,(也)像细丝,(它)(那么)密密地斜织着,(以至于)屋顶上全笼着一层薄烟。

又如马致远的《天净沙·秋思》:"枯藤老树昏鸦,小桥流水人家,古道西风瘦马,夕阳西下,断肠人在天涯。"整首词作为一个语篇,没有时间的提示,没有逻辑意思的衔接,几乎全是名词,只有两个表动作方位的词"西下"和"在天涯"。但整首词意思连贯,富有感染力,完全依靠读者对词中所描述的各种事物和人之间的联想,由物联想到人,从而感悟其中的思想感情。

从上述例句可见,重直觉和悟性的思维必然导致语言的高度简约化,而语言的高度简约化又会反过来要求读者（或听者）具有语言直觉和悟性，久而久之就形成了思维风格的传承。

2. 悟性思维导致汉语表述的广泛模糊化

模糊化主要表现为：词性模糊化——汉语很多词的词性并不清楚，如"动作"可作名词也可作动词；语义模糊化——如"中央和地方"中的"地方"，界定不明确，到底是省，是市，还是一种统称；句法成分模糊化——汉语中常常难以确定主、谓、宾、定、状、补等句子成分，如"谁有闲工夫打听这件事"这句话，到底是"有闲工夫"做"打听"的状语，还是"打听"做"有闲工夫"的补语，语法学家尚未给出定论；单复句界定的模糊化——如"我并没有做什么大事，不过做了应该做的事"这句是单句还是复句，语法学家们也是各持己见，纷争不已；动词形态的模糊化——如汉语动词没有时态、语态、语气这些形态标志。正因为以上种种模糊化，也导致了汉语语法的隐含性。

3. 歇后语的运用也是悟性思维的表现

歇后语是中国民间智慧的产物，是汉语特有的现象，其他语言鲜有。歇后语通常由前段和后段构成，二者有意义上的关联，但在实际运用时，说话者常隐去后段，只道出前段，要求读者或听话人从前段文字自己悟出后段内容，从而形成一种思维上的弹跳，这也是悟性思维的一种体现——要求别人去顿悟，如八仙过海——各显神通，泥菩萨过河——自身难保，肉包子打狗——有去无回，风吹灯草——心不定。

（二）英美民族的理性思维

自从古希腊哲学家亚里士多德开创了形式逻辑以后，形式逻辑与理性主义就对英美民族的思维习惯产生了深远的影响。理性思维重逻辑理念，在语言上的主要表现如下文所述。

1. 英语重形合

形合就是用各种语言形式手段，如形态变化、连接词等，表达语法和逻辑关系等。它是英语表达法的重要特点之一，使得英语语言形式呈现出严谨的组织化程度。试比较以下汉英翻译，可见英语重形合的倾向：

原文：日复一日，这种苦真使我对生活绝望了，我不想再干了，就偷懒、就哭泣，后来，头儿就让我去设在小村边上的一个仓库看库房，黑天白天都我一个人，吃饭时有人送来。

译文：Day in and day out, I had to do such hard toil so that I dropped into the depth of hopelessness. Thoroughly sick and tired of the job, I dawdled and wept while thus engaged. Later the leader of my team was kind enough to transfer me to be the keeper of a warehouse on the edge of the village. I was all alone twenty-four hours a day, even with my meals sent over to me.

分析：汉语原文中八个逗号，把各个分句隔开。句子中只有三个"就"和表示时间的"后来"和"吃饭时"，分句间没有什么逻辑关系可言，但意思依然连贯。

再看英语译文。因为英语的形合特性，要求英语句子通过一些连接手段在形式上和逻辑上把句子连接成句，不能像汉语那样，可以"一逗到底"，因此变成了四个句子。第一句，加了 so that 表示"我对生活绝望"和"这种苦"之间有着逻辑上的因果关系，"这种苦"造成了"我对生活绝望"这一结果；第二句中 "Thoroughly sick and tired of the job" 是说明我 dawdled and wept 的原因，对原文的理解成了由于"我不想再干了"，我"就偷懒，就哭泣"，英语中进一步说明了"我不想再干了"与"就偷懒，就哭泣"之间的逻辑关系。

2. 英语语法讲究精确性

精确性是西方近代思维方式的一大特征。理性的严密推理往往从命题出发，英语基本句型中主语和谓语缺一不可，正是形式逻辑基本命题的需要。另外，英语的语法具有显性的特征，强调形式上的完整清晰，各种语法成分之间的关系必须通过形式准确地标定，如并列关系、从属关系、指代关系等。

例：And then there was another Sunday and we were at Beon again that Sunday, and Russia came into the war and Poland was smashed and I did not care about Poland, but it frightened me about France.

分析：此英语句由三个并列分句组成。第一个分句由两个并列句（以 and 连接）构成；第二个分句以 and 连接第一个分句，且其自身由三个并列句（以 and 连接）构成；第三个分句用 but 表转折，其主语、谓语、宾语齐全。整个英语句子结构完整清晰，语法准确连贯，表意明确。

从以上例句可知，英语是融理性思维与严谨的语言结构于一体的典范。

三、主体与客体

中国文化注重主体性叙述，西方文化倾向于客体性描述，这是中西思维差异的重要方面之一。主体性是指以人为中心来观察、分析和研究客观世界，以主体意向来统摄客观事实，主体介入客体，客体融入主体，寓客观自然于主观价值判断之中。

中国人习惯从自我出发来理解、演绎客观事物，认为世上所有行为和事情都是由人这个行为主体来完成的。正如孟子所言："万物皆备于我。"在人（主体）与自然（客体）的关系上，中国人强调天人合一、物我一体，"宇宙便是吾心，吾心便是宇宙"，人与自然不是对立分明的关系而是和谐统一的整体，认识了自己也就认识了客观世界。因此，汉语思维是一种一元的主体意向性思维。

比较之下，西方民族主张"主客二分"，划分自我意识和认识对象，把人的内心世界和自然物象加以区别，既有主体性思维，也有客体性思维，但更加倾向于后者。因为西方人在把自然环境看作人类的对立面加以征服和改造的过程中，逐渐把客观世界当作探索、分析和研究的中心，甚至把人本身也作为客观世界的一部分加以研究。他们重视外向探索，强调客观作用及其对人的思想和行为的影响，常常把视点聚焦于外界事物而不是观察者本人，逐渐形成了客体对象占主导地位的思维方式。

主体性和客体性这两种不同的思维方式反映在语言上的明显差别之一，是在阐述事理和描述行为的过程中，汉语常使用人称主语，而英语常使用非人称主语。

四、具体与抽象

中国古代哲学讲究"观物取象""立意于象"，即从具体形象中把握、认识客观事物的规律。《易经》中的六十四卦均由图像表意，象征天、地、人之间的关系。《中庸》中提出"故君子尊德性而道学问，致广大而尽精微"，这里的"尽精微"

就是指明辨具体的分析。这些说明了中国人自古以来就注重具象思维，受此影响，汉语表达倾向于具体化、形象化。

作为一门"具象艺术"，汉字以"象形"作为主要构字方式，模仿自然界万物之形而构成，是具象思维的最好佐证。同时，汉语用词倾向于具体，常常以实的形式表达虚的概念，以具体的形象表达抽象的内容。很多成语，如生死之交、赤胆忠心、画饼充饥、种瓜得瓜、种豆得豆等，都是用具体的形象描摹来表达字面以外的深邃意境。

相较而言，西方文化崇尚理性、知性精神，表达倾向于概念化、抽象化。远起古希腊时期柏拉图的"理念世界"、亚里士多德的"形式逻辑"，近至17世纪培根的"经验哲学"、笛卡尔的"欧陆理性主义"，西方先哲们都擅长以数字、符号为工具，运用概念、判断、推理等思维形式，对客观现实进行间接的、概括的反映，使人们获得超出依靠感觉器官直接感知的知识，从感性的具体上升到理性的抽象。

具象思维要求取象与取义相结合，特定的思想要寄寓于具体的物象之中，并通过由此及彼的类别联系和意义涵摄，借助具象表达情感，以情感人。抽象思维是在对事物进行分析、综合和比较的基础上，从纷繁复杂的表面现象中提炼出事物的本质，由部分上升到整体，以严密的逻辑语句叙事说理，以理服人。东西方民族具象思维和抽象思维的差别明显地影响了文学作品的构思与表达。

第三节　英语翻译常用技巧

一、增译法

翻译的基本原则之一是译者不能随意增减原文信息。但由于英汉语言的思维方式、语言文字结构及表达习惯的差异，在翻译过程中有时需要补充某些必要的词语来衔接语义，增补可能出现的语义空缺，使译文更明确，合乎汉语的表达习惯，以达到和原文相似的修辞效果。增译可以把原文中隐含的内容，尤其是那些与原文背景相关的信息，用明显的语言形式表达出来，并没有增加意义，而是增加信息的凸显度。增译的原则是不能无中生有地随意增加语言单位，只是增加原文中虽无其形但有其意的一些语言单位。为使译文更加通顺达意，所增补的语言单位在修辞结构或语义上是必不可少的，增补后应无画蛇添足之感。

（一）增加原文省略的词语

英语中有些词在结构上或语义上可以省略而不影响意义的完整表达，但译成汉语后意义可能含糊不清。为使译文能明确表达原文，需要在翻译时添加被省略的词。

例1：She came to her work once a week—sweeping, scrubbing and cleaning.

译文：她每周来干一次活儿——扫地，擦地板，收拾房间。

分析：译文根据汉语的表达习惯在动词后增加了常搭配的宾语。

例2：We won't give up; we never have and never will.

译文：我们不会放弃，我们从没放弃过，将来也绝不放弃。

例3：Matter can be changed into energy, and energy into matter.

译文：物质可以转化成能量，能量也可以转化成物质。

分析：例2和例3的译文都增加了原文在结构上省略的成分。

（二）增加必要的连接词

英汉句法结构不同。英语往往在小句的基础上通过分词短语、不定式短语、介词短语等附加成分表示"时间、原因、条件、让步"等状语意义，还有一些无连接词的并列句，只用一定的标点符号隔开。翻译成汉语时必须根据其所暗含的意义、关系增加相应的关联词语。

例1：Heated, solids will change into liquids.

译文：固体如果加热，就会变成液体。

分析：原文是-ed分词作条件状语，译文中增加了表示条件的连词。

例2：He made many mistakes, bad ones.

译文：他犯了很多错误，而且还是很糟糕的错误。

分析：译文增加了承上启下的连词。

例3：Dark surfaces absorb heat; shining surfaces reflect it.

译文：黑暗的表面吸收热，而发光的表面反射热。

分析：原文前后为并列分句，意思上构成对比，译文增加"而"，凸显两者间的对比关系。

（三）增加表达复数概念的词语

英译汉时，有些情况下名词复数不译出来会引起误解，或有强调数量的必要，或根据汉语的表达习惯需要说明数量关系，此时在译文中需要增加表示数量关系的词语予以明确。

例1：Note that the words "velocity" and "speed" require explanation.

译文：请注意，"速度"和"速率"这两个词需要解释。

分析：译文增加了数量词"两个"，使语气更完整，表达更清晰。

例2：In spite of difficulties, he succeeded in finishing the task as scheduled.

译文：尽管困难重重，他如期成功地完成了任务。

分析：汉语中常用叠字来表达英语的复数概念。

（四）增加表达时间概念的词语

英语有各种时态，而汉语没有这一特点。因此，要在汉语译文中体现动作发生的时间，就要增加时间状语。

例1：I had never thought I'd be happy to find myself considered unimportant. But this time I was.

译文：以往我从来没想过，当我发现人们认为我无足轻重时，我会感到高兴。但这次情况确实如此。

分析：译文中增加了强调过去状态的词语。

（五）增添隐含主语

英语抽象名词用法简练，单个抽象名词往往内含一个动宾结构或主谓结构，隐含了施动者或作用者，翻译时要把隐含内容增添出来。

（1）Advertising campaigns have, however, promoted a growing realization of the advantages of these small plastic cards.

然而，广告公司的宣传活动，让越来越多的人相信这种小塑料卡的好处。

realization 是一个抽象名词。这里的 a growing realization of 意思是 people are increasingly realizing that ... 所以把主语增添出来。

（2）The future, then, to which the epoch of modern economic growth is leading is one of never ending economic growth, a world in which ever growing abundance is matched by ever rising aspiration.

现代经济发展时代所要引向的未来是一个经济发展永不停止的时代，是一个物质不断丰富、人们的愿望永不满足的世界。

这里的 abundance 和 aspiration，相应的形容词和动词是 abundant 和 aspire。和这两个词的经常搭配，前者是"物质"，后者是"人"，因此要翻译出这个意思。

【练习1】翻译下列各句，注意在原文基础上适当增加词汇。

1. Mother in-law is always on the side of her son, right or wrong.
2. Mary washed for a living after her husband had died of lung cancer.
3. The high-altitude plane was and still is a remarkable bird.
4. Nuclear radiation has a certain mystery about it, partly because it cannot be detected by human senses.
5. Mary looked older than her age, for she had had a hard life.
6. Mary is your friend as much as she is mine.
7. He ate and drank, for he was exhausted.
8. I knew it quite well as I know it now.
9. Oxidation will make iron and steel rusty.

二、省译法

增加和省略在翻译中可以互为补充，相辅相成。原文有所省略，译文就应当有所增补；若原文太过繁复，译文就当有所取舍。与增译法不能随意增加原文信息的原则相对应，运用省译法的前提是保证原文语义完整、信息准确。汉语以"意合"为特征，英译汉时，如果将原文中必不可少的词语和结构逐一翻译出来，有时会不符合汉语表达习惯或使译文显得累赘，因此在翻译的过程中要将一些原文需要而译文中却是多余的词语或结构加以省略。

（一）语法性省略

英语中有些词大多是因为语法需要而出现，而汉语中并不需要这些词，可以在译文中省略不译，这些词主要包括代词、冠词、介词、连词，有时动词也可以省略。

1. 代词的省略

一般说来，代词在英语中的使用要多于汉语。英译汉时，为了符合汉语的表达习惯，很多代词可以省略不译。

例1：If you drive a car, you must wear your seat belt.

译文：如果你开车，就必须系安全带。

例2：He put his hands into his pockets and then shook his head.

译文：他把双手插进口袋，然后摇了摇头。

例3：We live and learn.

译文：活到老，学到老。

分析：上述三个例句在译文中分别省略了人称代词 you，物主代词 your，his，泛指的人称代词 we。

2. 冠词的省略

汉语中没有冠词，英译汉时冠词往往可以省略。

例1：The sun was slowly rising above the sea.

译文：太阳慢慢从海上升起。

例2：The parties to a contract are the individuals or groups concerned.

译文：签署合同的各方是相关的个人或团体。

例3：Water changes from a liquid to a solid when it freezes.

译文：水结冰时从液体变成固体。

分析：例1、例2和例3中的冠词或表示独一无二的事物，或表示类别，均可省略不译。

但是带有明显指示意义的定冠词 the 和带有明显地表示"一个""一种"等意义的不定冠词 a（an）不可省略。

例1：The old man left without saying a word.

译文：那个老人一句话不说就走了。

分析：the 表特指，a 指"一"，译文中不可省略。

例2：The taxis driver gets a dollar a mile.

译文：计程车司机每开一英里就赚一块钱。

分析：the 表类别，译文中省略不译；两个 a 都指"一"，不能省译。

例3：Those girls are almost of an age.

译文：这些姑娘几乎都是同岁。

分析：an 指"一"，不可省略。

3. 介词的省略

汉语简洁明了，对介词的运用不如英语那么频繁。英译汉时，表示时间、地点的介词，尤其是时间、地点在译文中置于句首时，大都可以省略。

例1：Smoking is not allowed in the storehouse.

译文：仓库重地，禁止吸烟。

例2：In London in 1953 smog caused some 2000 deaths.

译文：1953年，伦敦有2000人左右死于烟雾。

例3：Now complaints are heard in all parts of the province.

译文：该省各地目前怨声载道。

表示地点的介词如果置于动词之后，在译文中一般不能省略。

4. 连词的省略

总体说来，英语重形合，词与词、短语与短语、句子与句子之间的关系主要通过连词表达。汉语重意合，词与词之间的关系大多靠词序加以体现，彼此的逻辑关系经常是暗含的，句子与句子之间的关系虽然常借助于连词来表达，但有时也可不用连词而依靠句序体现出来。正因为两种语言之间存在的这一差异，英汉翻译时原文中的不少连词经常省略不译或使用副词表达连接关系。以下分别举例说明并列连词与从属连词的省略：

（1）并列连词的省略

在并列连词中，比较常见的是 and、or、but 和 for 的省略，例如：

① He looked gloomy and troubled.

他看上去有些忧愁不安。

② This machine has worked in succession for seven or eight hours.

这台机器已经连续运转七八个小时了。

③ Bacteria, even great in number, are invisible to the unaided eye, but they can easily be distinguished by the microscope.

细菌即使为数甚多，肉眼也是看不见的，借助于显微镜却容易辨认出来。

④ Both the earth and grain of sand are bodies, for each consists of a definite amount of matter.

地球和砂粒都是物体，都是由一定数量的物质组成的。

（2）从属连词的省略

与并列连词相比，从属连词数量要大得多，用法也繁杂得多。无论是时间状语从句、原因状语从句、条件状语从句，还是起各种语法作用的名词性从句，均需相应的连词引导，汉译时这些连词经常可酌情省略。

首先，可以省略表示原因的连接词，因为英语一般需要用从属连词表示因果关系，而汉语则可以通过词序先后表示因果关系，例如：

① Because everyone uses language to talk, everyone thinks he can talk about language.

人人都用语言交谈，人人也就自认为能够谈论语言。

② Because the departure was not easy, we made it brief.

告别这件事情让人伤感，我们就此匆匆而别。

③ We knew spring was coming, as we had seen a robin.

我们看到了一只知更鸟，知道春天快要到了。

其次，可以省略表示条件的连接词。表示条件的从属连词 if、provided（that）

一般译为"如果""假如"等，但有时按照汉语行文习惯，可以省略不译。

① A gas becomes hotter if it is compressed.

气体受压缩，温度就升高。

② If winter comes, can spring be far behind?

冬天来了，春天还会远吗？

③ The volume of a given weight of gas varies directly as the absolute temperature, provided the pressure does not change.

压力不变，一定重量的气体的体积与绝对温度成正比。

最后，可以省略表示时间的连接词，因为在汉语中如果时间先后次序明显，为了简洁，往往可以省略这些连词。

① Check the equipment before you begin the experiment.

检查好设备再开始做实验。

② After he packed up his things, he hurried to the station.

他收拾好行李，急忙奔向火车站。

5. 动词的省略

英语注重语言形式，句子中必须有谓语动词；而汉语是一种意合连接的语言，语法结构不如英语那么严格。在英译汉过程中，谓语动词有时省略不译往往更符合汉语的表达习惯。这些能够在翻译过程中被省略的动词，主要是一些连系动词、一些与具有动词含义的名词搭配使用的动词。

例1：The new machine will prove useful to humankind.

译文：这个新机器会对人类有用。

例2：She had uncombed hair, dirty dress, and only 50 cents in her handbag.

译文：她头发凌乱，裙子肮脏，手提包里只有 50 美分。

例3：Delivery must be effected as scheduled.

译文：必须在规定的时间内交货。

分析：前两个例句中的动词都是连系动词，例 3 中的动词与含有动词含义的名词 delivery（传送、投递）搭配，都可省略不译。

（二）语义性省略

在进行英汉翻译时，有些词即使不翻译出来意思也很明确，翻译出来反而显得多余或是不符合汉语的表达习惯，此种情形下，需要采用省译法。

例1：Today, a good part of people suffers from malnutrition or from undernourishment.

译文：如今，有相当一部分人营养不良或营养不足。

分析：此句若译成"如今，有相当一部分人承受着营养不良或营养不足的痛苦"会显得累赘，省略后译文更简洁明了。

例2：What would happen if the population were to continue doubling in volume every 50 years?

译文：假如世界人口每50年翻一番，情况会怎样？

分析：如果将 in volume 在译文中翻译出来会显得多余。

例3：Job applicants who had worked at a job would receive preference over those who had not.

译文：有工作经验的求职者优先录取。

分析：译文中省略了 over those who had not，比译成"有工作经验的求职者比没工作经验的求职者优先录取"简洁，更符合汉语的表达习惯。

【练习2】翻译下列各句，注意适当省略原文中的词汇。

1. She glanced at her watch; it was 11:30.

2. You should not show your hand to a stranger.

3. The audience saw the little party climb ashore.

4. Rumors have already spread along the streets and lanes.

5. I framed the words in my mind: "Pardon me, but have I done something to offend you?"

6. When the pressure gets low, the boiling point becomes low.

7. Everywhere you can find new types of men and objects in New China.

8. Because the departure was not easy, we made it brief.

9. He studied in college for two years, and then he went to join the army.

10. Solids expand and contract as liquids and gases do.

三、词性转换

（一）名词与动词互转

1. 名词转动词

（1）具有动作含义的名词转译成动词，例如：

① He was accused of neglect of his duties.

他被指控玩忽职守。

② The sight and sound of our jet planes filled me with special longing.

看到我们的喷气式飞机，听到隆隆的机声，令我特别神往。

（2）动名词和由动词派生的名词往往转译成动词，例如：

① No other changes occur upon mixing the two compounds.

把这两种物质混合起来不会发生其他变化。

② In handling the materials of history, each act of selection is also an act of judgment.

在处理历史资料时，每选一项资料就是做出一种判断。

（3）由动词加后缀 -er 或 -or 构成的名词转译成动词。

英语中有些带后缀 -er 或 -or 的名词，有时在句中并不用来指某人的身份或职业，而是带有较强的动作含义。英语中所特有的这种语言现象在汉语中往往难以找到类似结构的词语与之对应加以表达。汉语中虽然也有由动词加后缀构成的名词，如"读者""驾驶员""清扫工"等，但这类名词主要用于指从事有关活动或职业的人，并不用来表示动作本身。因此，英语中这类名词在侧重表示动作意义时，一般宜转译为汉语动词。例如：

① Some of my classmates are good singers.

我的同学中有些人歌唱得很好。

② That well-known scientist was a great lover of literature when he was a child.

那位著名科学家小时候酷爱文学。

（4）在习语化短语动词中，作中心词的名词往往转译成动词。

英语中有大量习语化的短语动词，如 give a picture of, have a try, have a look at, have a rest, make mention of, pay attention to, take care of 等，它们的中心词是名词，译成汉语时，一般可以转换成动词，例如：

The lecturer gave an excellent picture of the living conditions in Africa.

讲演者生动地描绘了非洲的生活状况。

（5）其他名词转译成动词。

英语中有些名词尽管不具有明显的动作含义，但有时转译成汉语动词不仅有效地保持了原意，而且能使译文更加自然通顺，例如：

（1）A fire in the neighbor's house can easily bring disaster to everyone.

一家失火，四邻遭殃。

（2）Differences between the social systems of states shall not be an obstacle to their contact and cooperation.

各国社会制度不同，但不应妨碍彼此接触与相互合作。

2. *动词转名词*

同样，英语中有些动词很难按原词性翻译，需要用汉语中的名词对应，才能在意思表达上更为通顺。但英语动词转译汉语名词的情况较少。

（1）Before Jack London, the fiction dealing with the working class was characterized by sympathy for labor and the under privileged.

在杰克·伦敦之前，写工人阶级的小说都有这样的特点，即同情工人和穷人。

（2）He was motivated by a desire to reach a compromise.

他的动机是希望达成某种妥协。

（二）形容词与动词互转

英语形容词不少可以转译成动词。这种形容词大体包括两类：一类主要是由动词派生（或转换）而来，大多能引申出动作意义；另一类多用于表示各种心理状态，而这些心理状态在汉语中一般则用动词表达。

1. 形容词转换成动词

（1）由英语动词派生或转换成的形容词转译为汉语动词

形容词一般是属于静态的，主要用于表示人或事物的性质或状态等。但英语中的确有一部分形容词，尤其是那些由动词派生或转换来的形容词（即所谓的同源形容词），能够引申出动作意义。汉译时，这些形容词往往转换成动词，例如：

A solar cell is reproductive by itself under any circumstances.

太阳能电池在任何情况下都可以自行充电。

（2）表示某种心理状态的形容词转译成动词

英语中有一类表示知觉、感受、信念、欲望等心理状态的形容词，常出现在连系动词之后作表语，其后面大多要求与相应的介词搭配，或接不定式短语，或 that 从句。它们一般也具有动词的意义和特征，因而常常转译成汉语的动词，例如：

① The students are afraid that this chemical reaction will take place with great violence.

学生们担心，这个化学反应会以很强烈的方式发生。

② Scientists are quite confident that all the matters are indestructible.

科学家们深信物质是不灭的。

2. 动词转换成形容词

英语动词翻译为汉语形容词的情况较少，如：

I wonder if the play works in such a condition.

我在想这个计划在这样的条件是否有效。

（三）名词与形容词互转

1. 名词转换成形容词

一般说来，由形容词派生出来的名词，即以 -ness、-ity 等结尾的词都可转为形容词。

① We deeply convinced of the correctness of this policy and firmly determined to pursue it.

我们深信这一政策是正确的，并有坚定的决心继续奉行这一政策。

② Australian guests are immensely impressed by the splendor and warmth of our reception at the airport.

澳大利亚客人被我们在机场所给予的盛大、热情的接待深深感染了。

2. 形容词转换成名词

由名词派生过来的形容词，翻译时可以转换成汉语的名词。

① They expect us in the Community to work out policies of aid and trade which show a sympathetic understanding of their own problems.

他们期待欧洲共同体制定出对他们的问题表示同情和理解的援助政策和贸易政策。

从上面的例子可以看到，词类转换一般在派生词之间转换，只要意思一样，派生词之间的词类转换是可行的，correct → correctly → correctness。

【练习3】翻译下列各句。

1. Most countries of the world have a desire to mutually expand their trade.

2. "Coming!" Away she skimmed over the lawn, up the path, up the steps, across the veranda, and into the porch.

3. Talking with her daughter, the old woman was the forgiver of the young girl's past wrong doings.

4. But this very formulation is indicative of the underlying attitude.

5. The cutting tools must be strong, tough, and hard.

6. Though we can't see it, there is air all around us.

7. Internally the earth consists of two parts, a core and a mantle.

8. Scientists have been trying hard to understand the mystery of the space.

9. The novel Gone with the Wind impressed her deeply.

10. The new governor earned some appreciation by the courtesy of coming to visit those orphans.

四、专有名词的翻译方法

（一）英译汉专有名字翻译技巧

英语中有许多专有名词，如人名、地名、民族名、企业团体、国际组织及各类科技词汇等，在汉语中没有现成的表达方式，因而需要采用一些特殊的方法来翻译。一般来说，人名、地名和民族名等都采用音译法来处理，即用发音与原文相近的汉字译出。以上几种专有名词均可参照商务印书馆出版的《英语姓名译名手册》《外国地名译名手册》《世界民族译名手册》以及各种英汉辞典译出，使之统一起来，以免造成不应有的混乱或误解，但是仍有一些具体情况需要区别对待。

第一，有些约定俗成的译名，不必按其发音重新译出，免得出现混乱不一的现象，例如：

New York 译成"纽约"，而不译成"新约克"

Paris 译成"巴黎"，而不译成"巴黎斯"

Hollywood 译成"好莱坞"，而不译成"好莱坞德"

Singapore 译成"新加坡"，而不译成"辛加坡"

Adam Smith（英国古典经济学家）译为"亚当·斯密"，不要译成"亚当·史密斯"

Conan Doyle（英国侦探小说家）译为"柯南·道尔"，不要译成"柯南·多尔"

Joseph Needham（英国科学史学者）译为"李约瑟"，不要译成"约瑟夫·尼德汉姆"

San Francisco 一般译为"旧金山"（也可译作"圣弗朗西斯科"，但不如前者通用）

第二，有些人名、地名有重复现象，为了区别同名异地异人，也按约定俗成的译法处理，例如：

Cambridge——剑桥（英国），坎布里奇（美国）

Fanny——范尼（男名），范妮（女名）

Jessy——杰西（男名），杰希（女名）

Regan——里根（美国前总统），里甘（美国前任财政部部长）

第三，有的地名也用意译和半音译半意译，因为其中全部或有一部分为普通名词，例如：

①意译

Oxford——牛津

Salt Lake City——盐湖城

Iceland——冰岛

Long Island——长岛

②半音译半意译

New Zealand——新西兰

Grand Forks——大福克斯

South Wales——南威尔士

④带有序数词或其他普通词语的人名也应半音译半意译，如：

Henry V——亨利五世

Charles I——查理一世

⑤有些影片名、小说名，可采用比较灵活的方法译出，以达到吸引观众的目的。比如，根据内容另起标题：

Oliver Twist——《雾都孤儿》

Waterloo Bridge——《魂断蓝桥》

Carve Her Name with Pride——《女英烈传》

Gone with the Wind——《飘》

Pretty Woman——《风月俏佳人》

Casablanca——《北非谍影》

Sleepless in Seattle——《西雅图夜未眠》

⑥国外企业、团体、国际组织及国家的名称大都全部或部分由普通名词构成，亦有统一的译法。有些译名查不出统一的译法，可以根据具体情况或音译或意译或采取音意结合的方式进行翻译，例如：

Canadian Imperial Bank of Commerce——加拿大帝国商业银行

Shell——壳牌石油公司

Standard Chartered Bank——渣打银行

Standard & Poor's——标准普尔

⑦一些企业或组织名称经常用缩略语表示，其译法不一，有的仍译其全称，有的简译、全译并存，也有少数音译、意译两可的。

A. 全译，例如：

UNESCO——联合国教育、科学及文化组织

WHO——世界卫生组织

B. 简译全译并存，例如：

ASEAN——东盟（东南亚国家联盟）

WTO——世贸组织（世界贸易组织）

C. 音译意译两可，例如：

OPEC——欧佩克或石油输出国组织

⑧有些地名也用来指代该地特产，翻译时要弄清其含义，音译并增词说明，例如：

Morocco——大写为"摩洛哥"，小写则指"摩洛哥山羊皮"

Brussels——大写为"布鲁塞尔"，小写则指"布鲁塞尔毛圈地毯"

China——大写为"中国"，小写则为"瓷器"

⑨值得注意的是，有些英美名著、典故和神话传说中的人名、地名经过长期的沿用和演变，已具有普通名词的含义，或者说具有了比喻义，因此首先要理解其含义后再采取适当的方法译出。例如，可用音译加注的方法或意译：

Cinderella 可译为"灰姑娘"或"仙度里拉"（童话人物，喻义：不受重视的人）。

Uncle Tom 可译为"逆来顺受的人"或"汤姆叔叔"（《汤姆叔叔的小屋》中的人物，一个逆来顺受的人）。

Eden 可译为"乐园"或"伊甸园"（《圣经》中的地名乐园）。

Catch-22可译为"无法逾越的障碍"或"第二十二条军规"（来源于美国一部小说《第二十二条军规》，这是一条使人左右为难的军规）。

⑩有些专有名词甚至可以转译成动词：

to Richard Nixon——偷偷将录音抹掉

to Bond a thriller——拍一部詹姆士·邦德（系列侦探片《007》的主角）式的惊险片

to Bill Clinton——作伪证

to Hamlet——拿不定主意

to Shlock——放高利贷

⑪有些由专有名词与普通名词组成的词语具有特定的含义，千万不能望文生义，应查阅字典或有关参考资料，找出其准确的译名，如：

French leave——不辞而别

India summer——小阳春

Italian hand——暗中干预

British warm——军用短呢大衣

Turkish delight——橡皮糖

Spanish moss——铁兰

American plan——（旅馆的）供膳制

Dutch auction——逐渐降价的拍卖

（二）汉译英专有名字翻译技巧

1. 人名

汉语中人名的英译一般采用汉语拼音的方法进行翻译，例如：

闻一多——Wen Yiduo（双名）

傅雷——Fu Lei（单名）

王力——Wang Li（单名）

多吉才让——Duojicairang（少数民族人名）

2. 地名

（1）普通地名

一般采用汉语拼音的方法进行翻译，例如：

北京——Beijing

长春——Changchun

（2）风景名胜

①含地名的情况：地名的"汉语拼音＋意译"的方式进行翻译，例如：

承德避暑山庄——Chengde Mountain Resort

洞庭湖——Dongting Lake

华清池——Huaqing Hot Spring

峨眉山——Emei Mountain

都江堰——Dujiangyan Weir

嵩山——Songshan Mountain

庐山——Lushan Mountain

乐山大佛——Large Leshan Buddha

②不含地名的情况：一般采用意译的方法，例如：

东方明珠塔——the Oriental Pearl Tower

芦笛岩——Reed Flute Cave

黄鹤楼——Yellow Crane Tower

灵隐寺——Temple of Soul's（Lingyin）Retreat

中山陵——Dr.Sun Yet-sen's Mausoleum

③不含地名的情况："意译＋增译"地名，例如：

三峡——the Three Gorges on the Yangtze River

莫高窟——Mogao Grotto in Dunhuang

3. 机构名

（1）国务院所属部、委员会、局、办公室、署（总局）分别译为 Ministry，Commission，Bureau，Office，Administration（Bureau），例如：

教育部——Ministry of Education

国家统计局——National Bureau of Statistics

国土局——Land and Resources Bureau

工商局——Industrial and Commercial Bureau

国务院港澳事务办公室——Hong Kong and Macao Affairs Office of the State Council

国务院侨务办公室——Overseas Chinese Affairs Office of the State Council

国家新闻出版署——National Press and Publication Administration

审计署——Auditing Administration

旅行游览总局——General Administration of Travel and Tourism

（2）其他政府和群众组织如联合会、协会、大会、会议、委员会、出版社、法院、银行（信用社）等分别译为 Federation, Association, Congress, Conference, Committee, Press（Publishing House）, Court, Bank（Credit Cooperative），例如：

中华全国总工会——All-China Federation of Trade Unions

中华全国妇女联合会——All-China Women's Federation

中国残疾人联合会——China Disabled Persons' Federation

省（自治区）人民代表大会——Provincial（Autonomous Regional）People's Congress

市人民代表大会——City People's Congress

商务印书馆——Commercial Press

4. 称谓和技术职称

第一，在汉语中，首席长官的称谓常常以"总……"表示，在英语中表示首席长官的称谓则常常带有 chief, general, head, managing 这类词。在汉译英时，要遵循英语的表达习惯，例如：

总工程师——chief engineer

总编辑——chief editor; editor-in-chief; managing editor

总经理——general manager, managing director; executive head

总裁判——chief referee

总代理——general agent

第二，在汉语中，有些机构或组织的首长在英语中有特殊的表达，例如：

某大学校长——President of XX University

某中小学校长——Principal/Headmaster of XX Middle School

某大学二级学院院长——Dean ofthe XX School

某大学二级学院系主任——Chair/Chairman of the XX Department

某学会/协会的会长/主席——President of the XX Association

某工厂厂长——Director of the XX Manufacturing Plant

某医院院长——President of XX Hospital

第三，汉语中有些机构的负责人可以用 director，head 或 chief 来表示。如：司（department）、厅（department）、署（Office）、局（bureau）、所（institute）、处（division）、科（section）、股（section）、室（office）、教研室（section）等的负责人。

第四，汉语中表示副职的头衔一般都带"副"字，翻译成英语时需要视词语的固定搭配或表达习惯而定。在英语中可供选择的词有 vice、associate、asistant、deputy 等。

比较而言，vice 和 associate 使用的频率较高，前者一般用于行政职务的副职，后者一般用于学术头衔，例如：

副部长——vice minister

副省长——vice governor

副市长——vice mayor

副领事——vice consul

中小学副校长——vice principal

副教授——associate professor

第五，assistant 一般用于以下职位的副职和初级技术职称，例如：

经理助理——assistant manager

中小学副校长——assistant headmaster

助理教授——assistant professor

助理研究员——assistant research fellow

助理工程师——assistant engineer

第六，deputy 一般用于以下职位的副职，例如：

副所长 / 副厂长 / 副主任——deputy director

大学二级学院副院长——deputy dean

副市长——deputy mayor

副秘书长——deputy secretary-general

第七，有的行业的高级职称用"高级"或"资深"来表示，译成英语时习惯上用 senior，例如：

高级工程师——senior engineer

高级讲师——senior lecturer

高级教师——senior teacher

高级记者——senior reporter

高级农艺师——senior agronomist

高级编辑——senior editor

第八，有的带有"首席"的行业职称，英语习惯上用 chief 来表示，例如：

首席执行官——chief executive officer（CEO）

首席仲裁员——chief arbitrator

首席顾问——chief advisor

首席记者——chief correspondent

审判长——chief judge；chief of judges；presiding judge

第九，带有"代理"的职务，一般用 acting 来译，例如：

代理市长——acting mayor

代理主任——acing director

第十，带有"常务"的职务，一般用 managing 来译，例如：

常务副市长——managing vice mayor，first vice mayor

常务副校长——managing vice president；first vice president

常务理事——managing director

第十一，带有"执行"的职务，一般用 executive 来译，例如：

执行秘书——executive secretary

执行主任——executive director

第十二，带有"名誉"的职务，一般用 honorary 来译，例如：

名誉教授——honorary professor

名誉院长——honorary dean

第十三，有的职称或职务是"……长""主……""主治……""特级……""特……""特派……"译成英语时要视英语的表达习惯而定，例如：

护士长——head nurse

秘书长——secretary-general

参谋长——chief of staff

检察长——prosecutor-general

主任医师——senior doctor

第十四，汉语的许多职称、职务的英语表达法难以归类，需要不断积累记忆，例如：

财务主任——treasurer

编审——senior editor；professor of editorship

院士——academician

博士生导师——doctoral student supervisor

研究生导师——graduate student tutor

第十五，有些中国特有的荣誉称号在英语中无法找到对应的表达，多用意译的方法来翻译，例如：

三好学生——"triple-A" outstanding student；outstanding student

劳动模范——model worker

练习参考答案

第二章　英语阅读学习策略与指导

第三节　阅读训练

Reading 1

Passage One

1.D　2.B　3.B　4.C　5.D

Passage Two

1.D　2.D　3.A　4.B　5.A

Reading 2

1.C　2.A　3.B　4.D　5.D

Reading 3

1.A　2.C　3.C　4.B　5.D

Reading 4

1.C　2.D　3.B　4.D　5.A

第三章　英语写作学习策略与指导

第一节　句子写作

练习 1

1. On the plane I heard the joke which did not amuse me at all.

2. My classmate had helped me. My classmate helped me to find some interesting books that I had lost a week before.

3. I will attend the class because I like the teacher's lecture.

4. A high mountain out of the window blocked my view.

5. He is called James Bond.

6. Where he goes, he visits all the places of interest there.

7. The whole class elected Liu their monitor.

8. She is not only a famous singer but also a super dancer.

9. Tom is earnest, responsible and honest. You can trust him.

10. He drank a cup of tea and read a newspaper at the table.

练习2

Exercise One

1. The police are looking for the escaped prisoner.（主语 the police 是集合名词）

2. The number of girl students in the English Department is great.（主语是 the number）

3. A number of foreigner scholars were invited to the anniversary celebration of our university.（主语是 scholars）

4. Nowadays news is translated instantly to mass audiences.（主语 news 是不可数名词）

5. Physics is taught by a Mr. Smith.（主语 Physics 是一门学科）

Exercise Two

1. Either Bill or John will bring a sample of his own work.（先行词是 John）

2. Jane and Jill called their friend.（先行词是 Jane and Jill）

3. Either Mary or her friends will present their design.（先行词是 her friends）

4. Every employee wants to impress their employer.（先行词 every, employee 相当 all employees）

5. Each of the boys had his homework finished.（先行词是 each）

Exercise Three

1. Although a lifetime is short, much can be accomplished.

2. In spite of the fact that Jane Martin had a speech defect, she became a great professor.

3. When they are in doubt, most drivers apply the brakes.

4. The government was considerably weakened because corruption in high places became widespread.

5. While Gary was taking a shower, he thought of a great idea.

6. Nobody knew why Mr. Martin left his office early.

7. Although the final examination was easy, he passed with a low grade.

8. Our biology professor has written that book with the bright red cover.

Exercise Four

1. It began to rain heavily at 9 o'clock last night.（rain 为延续动词，与"at+时间点"不能连用）

2. Shakespeare was one of the greatest dramatists in the world.（缺少最高级的范围）

3. Many people in that region believe that one should eat garlic everyday to prevent disease.（介词短语修饰语要尽量靠近其修饰的名词）

4. The soil erosion damaged a few houses only.（only 在此表示房屋损失的程度，而不是泥石流本身的危害）

5. Most students in our class chose chemistry instead of physics.（chemistry 不能作 taking physics 的主语）

Exercise Five

1. The gardener who had cut the weeds thought about the vacation planned for August.（定语从句）

a. Having cut the weeds, the gardener thought about the vacation planned for August.（分词短语作状语）

b. As he cut the weeds, the gardener thought about the vacation planned for August.（原因状语从句）

c. The gardener cut the weeds and thought about the vacation planned for August. （并列句）

2. When they saw the curtain go up, the audience gasped in surprise and started applauding loudly. （时间状语从句）

a. <u>Seeing the curtain go up</u>, the audience gasped in surprise and started applauding loudly. （分词短语作时间状语）

b. The audience <u>saw</u> the curtain go up, <u>gasped</u> in surprise <u>and started</u> applauding loudly. （简单句含三个并列谓语动词）

3. The man was looking forward to living an easy life in Canada after he had amassed a fortune. （时间状语从句）

a. <u>Having amassed a fortune</u>, the man was looking forward to living an easy life in Canada. （分词短语作时间状语）

b. Having amassed a fortune, the man was looking forward to living an easy life in Canada.

4. She hurried down to the bank, withdrew all her savings, and gave them to her mother. （简单句含三个并列谓语动词）

a. <u>Hurrying down to the bank</u>, she withdrew all her savings and gave them to her mother. （第一个谓语动词变成分词短语作时间状语）

b. <u>After she hurried down to the bank and withdrew all her savings</u>, she gave them to her mother. （前两个谓语分离出来作时间状语从句的并列谓语）

c. She hurried down to the bank, withdrew all her savings <u>which she gave to her mother</u>. （把最后一个谓语分离出来作定语从句的谓语）

5. The new recruits lined up rapidly, and the officers gave them their orders for the day. （并列句）

a. <u>Having lined up rapidly</u>, the recruits were given their orders for the day. （第一个并列分句变成分词短语，突出"新兵接受命令"）

b. <u>After the new recruits lined up rapidly</u>, the officers gave them their orders for the day. （第一个并列分句变成时间状语从句）

c. The new recruits who had lined up rapidly were given their orders for the day.(第一个并列分句变成定语从句，突出"已经排好队的新兵接受命令")

d. The officers gave the new recruits who had lined up rapidly their orders for the day. (把第二个并列句放在句首，把第一个并列分句变成定语从句，突出"军官给已经排好队的新兵传达命令")

第二节　段落写作

练习 1

段落 1

Father's Day is a celebration of fathers inaugurated in the early twentieth century to celebrate fatherhood and male parenting. Modern Father's Day was invented by Sonora Smart Dodd, to honor her father, the Civil War veteran William Jackson Smart, a single parent who reared his six children. The first Father's Day was celebrated on June 19, 1910, in Spokane, Washington. From then on, people across America began to celebrate a "Father's Day". In 1924 President Calvin Coolidge supported the idea of a national Father's Day. Finally in 1966 President Lyndon Johnson signed a presidential proclamation declaring the third Sunday of June as Father's Day.

段落 2

Model A

The apartment I live in is on the third floor in a building near Ljiang. It is a 4-bedroom plus 2-bath ind 2-balcony apartment of 130 square meters. When you come into the apartment, first you see a large sitting room on your left, on your right is a bathroom, a kitchen and a small dining hall, a small room with a small balcony. Going seven steps upstairs, you come to the second floor. First you see a bathroom in your direction. On your let is a bedroom with a balcony, next to it is the other bedroom. On your right is the library. In the library, there are two desks besides the window, and two bookshelves against the wall facing the window, and there are another four bookshelves on the left against the wall. There are thousands of books in the bookshelves. Welcome to my home, and enjoy reading books in the library.

Model B

The dormitory I live in is on the fifth floor in Dormitory Building No.9. It is a room of about 12 square meters. When you get into the dorm, on your right, you will find two double-deck beds with two desks beside the first deck, on the left there are two more desks. Walking a few steps inside, there is the balcony where we do washing and hang our clothes, and next to the balcony is the washing room.

段落 3

Traffic accident is one of human beings' fatal enemies. The major cause for traffic accidents is the lack of safety awareness. Therefore, drivers should complete safety driving education courses and build up their self-conscience for safety driving, and the government should enhance people's safety awareness. In this way, safety-related traffic accidents will be reduced.

段落 4

Love is of three varieties: unselfish, mutual, and selfish. Unselfish love is of the highest kind. Here, the one who loves seeks only the welfare of the beloved and does not care whether he suffers pains and hardships thereby. The second kind of love is mutual love in which the one who loves desires not only the happiness of his beloved, but also has an eye to his own happiness. Selfish love is the lowest. It makes a man care only for his own happiness without having any regard for the feelings of the beloved.

第三节　篇章写作

练习 1

范文：

The Eve of My Departure for College

On the eve of my departure for college, there was a great fuss in my family. My mother prepared many dishes for a farewell party to which all family members were summoned, and that created a festive atmosphere.

It was the first time that I was to live away from home for as long as half a year. My parents were somehow a bit upset. Father gave me a great deal of advice as to my health and college career. He wanted me to write home at least once a week and consult him about any kind of trouble that I might be confronted with. He also gave me four letters which were to be delivered by me to his friends living in the city and intended for introducing me to them.

My mother packed a lot of things-even cakes and biscuits, among other things-in my luggage. She told me repeatedly how to take good care of myself on campus. My brother, aged eleven, offered to sleep in my bed together with me for the night and presented to me a picture of a dog. He said: "You will be quite a young man when you get back." As a response I encouraged him to be nice and obedient to my parents.

I went to bed after eleven o clock that night. My mind was so full of fantasies that I did not fall asleep till one o'clock. I thought of new friends I was going to make and of my sweet home I had to be absent from for half a year. I had a dream that night, and in the dream I see myself come back home six months later. While I see myself entering my house, I suddenly woke up. It was already half past seven in the morning. I got up at once to rush to the railway station for catching the train which was to take me to my college.

练习 2

范文:

The Harvest Time

Perhaps autumn is the most pleasant season of the year. The weather is neither too hot nor too cold. It is the best time for going to the countryside.

Last Sunday we went to the countryside. There was golden wheat all over the fields. There was a wood of fruit trees surrounded by the fields, in which large and colorful apples and pears were hanging heavy on the trees. We could see that some peasants were busy cutting the wheat in the fields, and others were picking fruits from the trees. All the baskets were full of lovely fruits. They are the reward to the hard work of the peasants.

I love the harvest time. Standing in the farm lands I felt that I was in a splendid fairyland.

练习 3

范文：

Opportunity and Success

In our life, we can often hear people complain that they don't have the opportunity to succeed. So they give up their effort and wait for opportunities but opportunities never come.

Yes. Opportunities are very important to our success and they don't come often. But they favor a ready mind. When an opportunity presents itself, it brings a promise but never realizes it on its own. If we want to achieve something or fulfill one of our ambitions we must work hard, make efforts and get prepared. Otherwise, we will not be able to take advantage of opportunities when they come to visit us.

The difference between those who succeed and those who do not lies only in the way they treat opportunities. The successful people always make adequate preparations to meet opportunities as they duly arrive. The unsuccessful people, on the other hand, just idle and wait to let opportunities slip past unnoticed. It is clear that the different attitudes towards opportunities can lead to different consequences.

In fact, there are plenty of opportunities for everyone in our society, but only those who are prepared adequately and qualified highly can make use of them to achieve success. Therefore, the secret of success is for a man to be ready for his opportunity when it comes.

练习 4

范文：

A Brief Introduction to the University

Distinguished guests,

Welcome to our university. Before you start to look around, allow me to give you a brief account of the university.

Founded in 1927, our university is one of this city's earliest universities of liberal arts. It is staffed with an excellent faculty, and has a total enrollment of over 10,000 students. In the past years, it has turned out numerous well-qualified students and found its graduates active in professions of all walks of life.

Since its establishment, the university has always steered itself toward the objective that its students have an overall healthy development. Not only does it provide the students with basic academic courses, but it manages to expose them to the up-to-date knowledge. Besides, students are free to participate in colorful campus activities and social practice, which are intended for broadening their mind and developing their potential talent.

Currently, both our faculty and students are making every effort to improve the quality.

第四章　英语语法学习策略与指导

第一节　英语语法概述

练习1

Ⅰ部分

1.G　2.F　3.A　4.C　5.F　6.E　7.B

Ⅱ部分

1. A：have thought about

   B：going into space

2. A：to choose her own friends

   B：Her parents

3. A：to solve all the problems

   B：with the time given

4. A：had been compelled

B：to give up much of his time：

Ⅲ部分

1.G 2.F 3.G 4.F 5.E 6.B 7.D 8.C

第三节 语法综合练习

1-5 C C A D C

6-10 B B C A D

11-15 B B B C B

16-20 A B C A D

21-25 B A D A D

26-30 B B B A C

31-35 C B D D C

36-40 B C B A C

41-45 A B A A B

46-50 C A C D C

第五章 英语翻译学习策略与指导

第三节 英语翻译常用技巧

练习1

1. 婆婆总是偏袒自己的儿子，不管他是对还是错。

2. 玛丽在丈夫患肺癌去世后靠洗衣服维持生活。

3. 这种高空飞机过去是、现在仍然是很好的飞机。

4. 核辐射这种现象多少有点神秘，其部分原因是人类感官无法觉察到它的存在。

5. 玛丽看起来比她实际的年龄要老一些，因为她曾经历过很艰苦的生活。

6. 玛丽既是你的朋友，又是我的朋友。

7. 他吃了点东西，喝了点酒，因为他疲惫不堪了。

8. 我在当时对这件事的了解就和现在一样清楚。

9. 氧化作用会使钢铁生锈。

练习2

1. 她一看表，十一点半了。

2. 对陌生人要存几分戒心。

3. 观众看见那一小队人爬上岸。

4. 各种流言蜚语早就传遍了大街小巷。

5. 我心里嘀咕："对不起，我做了什么事冒犯了你吗？"

6. 气压低，沸点就低。

7. 新中国处处可以看到新人、新事物。

8. 告别这件事难受得很，我们就做得简短一些。

9. 他在大学念过两年书，后来就去参军了。

10. 如同液体和气体一样，固体也能膨胀和收缩。

练习3

1. 世界上的大多数国家都希望扩展双方贸易。

2. "来啦！"她转身蹦蹦跳跳地跑了，越过草坪，跑上小径，跨上台阶，穿过阳台，进了门廊。

3. 在和女儿谈话时，老妇人宽恕了年轻女孩过去所干的坏事。

4. 但是这一说法本身就已表明其根本态度。

5. 刀具必须有足够的强度、韧性、硬度。

6. 虽然我们看不见空气，可我们周围到处都是空气。

7. 地球的内部由两部分组成：地核和地幔。

8. 科学家一直在努力地探索神秘的太空。

9.《飘》这部小说令她印象深刻。

10. 新州长有礼貌地前来看望这些孤儿，获得了他们的好感。

参考文献

[1] 邵帅.英语教学 大学英语口语教学理论与实践[M].北京：知识产权出版社，2017.06.

[2] 赵荣斌.多理论视角下的大学英语口语教学研究[M].北京：光明日报出版社，2016.08.

[3] 邢新影.大学英语口语教学理论与实践[M].长春：吉林出版集团有限责任公司，2009.06.

[4] 谢丽.外语教学指导与学术研究系列丛书大学英语阅读教学理论与实践研究[M].北京：北京理工大学出版社，2015.06.

[5] 吴杰荣，陈宝娣.问题式教学法在大学英语阅读教学中的应用研究[M].哈尔滨：东北林业大学出版社，2017.06.

[6] 张君棠.大学英语阅读教学理论与实践[M].北京：冶金工业出版社，2014.06.

[7] 王笃勤.大学英语阅读教学活动设计[M].哈尔滨：哈尔滨工程大学出版社，2011.05.

[8] 吴婷婷，宋洁，杨慧.大学英语写作教学研究[M].长春：吉林人民出版社，2021.09.

[9] 扈玉婷.大学英语生态化写作教学研究[M].北京：北京理工大学出版社，2019.03.

[10] 张冬梅.大学英语写作教学——以产出导向法为视角[M].长春：吉林大学出版社，2022.02.

[11] 黄耀华.基于语料库的大学英语写作教学研究[M].西安：西安交通大学出版社，2017.07.

[12]王瑞.大学英语写作教学档案袋评测研究[M].哈尔滨:黑龙江大学出版社,2016.11.

[13]姜涛.大学英语写作教学理论与实践[M].长春:吉林出版集团有限责任公司,2009.06.

[14]蒋云华.网络环境下大学英语写作教学理论与实践[M].昆明:云南大学出版社,2012.06.

[15]冯莉.大学英语语法教学理论与实践[M].长春:吉林出版集团有限责任公司,2009.06.

[16]全国大学英语四、六级考试委员.大学英语词汇、语法和综合技能测试与教学[M].上海:上海外语教育出版社,1997.04.

[17]河南省部分高等院校.大学英语四级教学辅助教材 词汇·语法·写作[M].郑州:河南人民出版社,1990.11.

[18]张道真.张道真大学英语语法[M].北京:世界图书出版公司,2020.04.

[19]刘淑颖.大学英语语法应用教程[M].西安:西安电子科技大学出版社,2018.02.

[20]董亚芳.大学英语语法与练习上[M].上海:上海外语教育出版社,2017.04.

[21]余玲.文学翻译与大学英语教学[M].北京:原子能出版社,2019.09.

[22]李朝,杨仲韬.大学商贸英语翻译教程教学参考书[M].上海:复旦大学出版社,2007.08.

[23]李霞.大学英语翻译与教学实践研究[M].西安:西北工业大学出版社,2020.08.

[24]大学英语翻译教学设计与应用[M].延吉:延边大学出版社,2019.07.

[25]大学英语翻译教学中的跨文化教育研究[M].北京:中国国际广播出版社,2019.11.

[26]张雪芳.关联理论与大学英语翻译教学研究[M].西安:西北工业大学出版社,2017.08.

[27]刘先林.大学英语教学策略研究[J].新商务周刊,2019(6):246.

[28]孙胜男."互联网+"下的大学英语教学策略探析[J].智库时代,2020(43):203,298.

[29]许瀚云.异文化背景下大学英语教学策略探究[J].校园英语,2021(20):42—43.

[30]许晓丽.多元智能理论指导下的大学英语教学策略分析[J].新一代,2021(20):51.